RAIL FACILITIES
ORANGE COUNTY
CALIFORNIA
Circa May 1928

Rails
through
the
Orange Groves

A Centennial look at the Railroads of Orange County, California

by Stephen E. Donaldson
William A. Myers

volume 2

TRANS-ANGLO BOOKS • Glendale, California 91225

Dedication

*To Nancy, Kristin, and Kevin, who
helped Steve through a tough time.
This volume has come to completion as
a direct result of their love and
devotion.*
*To Lynn, for her patience and
understanding yet again, and to
Leslee "Munchkin," for being
Daddy's girl.*

Front Cover

Bastanchury Crossing

*At only three places in Orange County
did the track of one railroad pass over
the track of another on separate grades.
One is illustrated here on the
Bastanchury Ranch in the Los Coyotes
Hills (now Sunny Hills) where the
lines of the Union Pacific and Pacific
Electric running between La Habra
and Fullerton crossed over one another.
One of PE's famous Red Cars carries a
pair of commuters across the bridge,
while a UP steamer pokes through
below, toting the day's quota of
refrigerated fruit and other freight
through the orange groves.*
— Painting by Pat Karnahan

Back Cover

*(Above) This 1910-era postcard shows a
celery farmer near Westminster tending his
field. This valuable crop brought prosperity
to many "peat lands" farmers in the years
following the turn of the century.*
— Courtesy Don Dobmeier

*(Below) In a splendid scene along the beach
at San Clemente, we find a seven-car San
Diegan southbound on the morning of
October 4, 1986. F40PH 222 is on the
point of Amtrak No. 572. After the
Northeast Corridor, this is the most highly
travelled passenger rail line in the United
States.*
— C.R. Prather

Frontispiece Photo

*Northern No. 3751 whisks a northbound
"San Diegan" past an orange grove
alongside Lincoln Avenue in Santa Ana,
circa 1951.*
— Marshall Nelson

Rails through the Orange Groves, Volume 2
A Centennial look at the Railroads of Orange County, California

© 1990 by Stephen E. Donaldson
William A. Myers
All Rights Reserved

Volume I edited by Paul Hammond
Volume II edited by Robert Willoughby Jones
Book design and layout by Jim Reese

Manufactured in the United States of America

First Printing: Fall 1990

Library of Congress Cataloging Data
(Revised for vol. 2)

Donaldson, Stephen E.
    Rails through the orange groves.
    Includes bibliographical references and indexes.
    1. Railroads – California – Orange County – History.
I. Myers, William A., 1947-   II. Title.
TF24.C3D66   1989   385'.09794   89-7619
ISBN O-87046-088-9 (v. 1)
ISBN O-87046-094-3 (v. 2)

ISBN 0-87046-094-3
Published by TRANS-ANGLO BOOKS a division of
INTERURBAN PRESS
P.O. Box 6444   Glendale, California 91225

Table of Contents

Volume Two

Acknowledgements

The authors wish to extend their sincere apologies to Pat Karnahan, the accomplished railroad artist who painted the dust jacket pictures for the first and second volumes of this work, and to cartographer Earnie Towler, who drew the local rail maps, for having inadvertently left their names out of the list of acknowledgements in the first volume. This embarassing oversight in no way mitigates the contribution.these two men made to the book. Thanks are also due to John Signor who drew the county-wide map and contributed several photographs from his vast archive.

This book was made possible only through the encouragement and cooperation of many historians, archivists, collectors and professional railroaders. So protracted has been the gathering of data that many of these individuals have since retired, transferred to other capacities, or, sadly, in some cases, passed away.

The authors wish to acknowledge the assistance of the following individuals and institutions: Orange County historians Don Meadows and Ed Miller; the late Gerry Best; Richard J. Fellows; the late Ira L. Swett; the Charles W. Bowers Museum in Santa Ana; the Los Angeles County Museum of Natural History; the Bancroft Library; the *Santa Ana Register*; the public libraries of Santa Ana, Newport Beach, Huntington Beach, Anaheim, Fullerton, Orange, Yorba Linda, Los Angeles, and San Diego; the libraries and special collections at U.C.L.A. and U.S.C.; Roger Berry, Special Collections Librarian, U.C. Irvine; the California Public Utilities Commission; the Interstate Commerce Commission; the California State Railroad Museum; Cynthia Swanson, Law Librarian, Southern California Edison Company; and various agencies of the County of Orange.

Particular and specific assistance was provided by Dr. William O. Hendricks, Director, Sherman Foundation Library; Andy Anderson, Assistant Vice President, Southern Pacific Transportation Company, San Francisco; Michael A. Martin, Santa Fe Southern Pacific Corporation; Joseph Strapac, Southern Pacific Historical & Technical Society; John Berry, Santa Fe Railway Historical Society; Derrell Brewer and Roger Simon, Southern California Chapter, Railway & Locomotive Historical Society; Tom Nelson and Ralph Melching, Pacific Railroad Society; William Garner, San Bernardino Railway Historical Society; Ted Parker and Priscilla Melenson, First American Title Company, Santa Ana; and Pete Kowney, Knotts Berry Farm.

Important information came from the personal collections of Ray Younghans, Dave Norris, Cliff Prather, Lee Gustaffson, Bruce Frenzinger, and Bruce Jones. Several local Orange County historical societies and historians also made materials available from their collections.

Thanks also to the numerous photographers and collectors, including members of the Orange County Railway Historical Society, who shared their materials to illustrate the book.

A special remembrance goes to Irene Gsovski, who years ago encouraged one of the authors to begin the original research which ultimately lead to this book.

To all, the authors express their deepest thanks for the generosity and shared enthusiasm.

Stephen E. Donaldson and William A. Myers
Orange County, 1990

Introduction to Volume Two

When the first volume of this book went to press in 1989, Orange County was celebrating its Centennial Anniversary. This event was more than just a milestone birthday, it was a coming of age for a geographically small yet economically muscular region. Residents county-wide used the Centennial to become more aware of their rich historical heritage which encompassed more than beach-side resorts, orange groves and a mission.

The authors were overwhelmed by the enthusiastic response with which the first volume of this work was met. Chapters on Orange County's industrial and agricultural heritage had been planned for the first volume, but were held back for reasons of space. This was fortunate, for the Centennial triggered an outpouring of new materials which now appear in this second volume.

As the authors noted in their introduction to the first volume of this history, the County's rail story does not conclude with a sad account of decline and abandonment, since three major railroad companies still provide an extensive freight service within Orange County, and Amtrak operates a passenger service that is second only to the Northeast Corridor in ridership. In the eighteen months since those words were written, little has changed. The Union Pacific, always a "distant third" among the county's rail carriers, has abandoned a short segment of its trackage into the heart of downtown Anaheim, but still operates an important service to La Habra and Fullerton. The Southern Pacific has abandoned about three miles of its original 19th-Century main line alignment in Anaheim and Santa Ana to accomodate a widening of the parallel Santa Ana Freeway, shifting its Santa Ana and Costa Mesa-bound freight trains to an increasingly crowded segment of the Santa Fe Railway.

The Santa Fe trackage in the County has been improved by the so-called LOSSAN Project. Double tracking, siding lengthening, signalling improvements, and rerailing have resulted in greater capacity for this heavily used main line. This increased capacity has made possible the addition of a greatly needed ninth round trip passenger train which began operating in April of 1990. Thanks to Amtrak's "push-pull" train technology now used on all trains in this corridor, the new train may shuttle between Los Angeles and San Juan Capistrano without requiring turning facilities. In addition, a new rail passenger station is soon to open to serve the Cities of Irvine and El Toro.

There is also a rising awareness among Orange County residents about the need to build new rail transit lines to help alleviate the County's worsening traffic problems. Although recent efforts to authorize transit taxes or bond sales have been turned down at the polls, these defeats were the result of strong public disagreement over the emotionally-charged issues of growth, land use, and highway construction, rather than due to an inherent disapproval of rail construction. The County's Transit District owns a portion of the former Pacific Electric Santa Ana line which could be used to provide a direct connection from the county seat to Los Angeles County's rail transit system, including direct rail access to Los Angeles International Airport. Other freight lines have been offered for sale by the railroads for transit purposes, and the Southern California Area Governments Association – a regional planning group – has identified other rail lines that should be acquired for transit purposes. The authors remain hopeful that before the turn of the century "light rail transit" (trolley cars) will return to Orange County. Who knows, they might even be painted red!

These developments indicate that railroads and rail technology continue to make important contributions to the economic and societal needs of Orange County.

Deciduous and semi-tropical fruits, especially citrus, were important sources of freight revenue on Southern Pacific's Tustin Branch. In this 1915 view of SP's Tustin depot, fruit from the field is being sorted and packed for shipment.
– First American Title Company

5 Celery, Sugar Beets and Citrus
Hauling Orange County Crops By Railroad

Further extension of Orange County's railroad network, the level of service provided by the railroads, and the composition of traffic over the lines were all determined primarily by the output of the county's farms. After the turn of the century, county agriculture and resulting rail shipments shifted from grain and livestock to more valuable field crops and fruit. Particularly significant during the first half of the Twentieth Century were celery, sugar beets and citrus, each of which successively produced heavy tonnages and contributed significantly to the county's rail history.

The Santa Ana and Westminster Railroad

Shipments of Orange County farm products by rail grew from 50,000 tons in 1896 to 150,000 tons ten years later. This growth in productivity was due to the planting of greater acreage in items of higher value and to the production of higher density crops. Higher value (but often very perishable) crops became attractive to county farmers only after the railroads demonstrated that they could ship such valuable products to market at speeds which would ensure arrival before spoilage occurred. The planting of higher density crops became possible because their great volume could be handled efficiently by railroads, which offered greater load-bearing and concentrating capacity than was available with other transportation technologies.

For some Orange County farmers, being endowed with soil or other natural resources of great economic potential was not enough; that potential could not be realized if the products of the area could not be shipped to market efficiently, competitively, and rapidly. A case in point was the district around Westminster. This was one of the earliest settled areas in the county and its rich peat soil became legendary for producing giant vegetables. Yet this area was unable to participate in the early economic growth of the county because of repeated delays in receiving direct railroad service.

Westminster was to have been included on the route of one of the earliest railroads proposed in the Santa Ana Valley — the Anaheim Railroad — incorporated in 1870 to build a narrow gauge line from Anaheim to Anaheim Landing. Before the enthusiasm of the promoters faded, they even talked of extending rails as far as San Bernardino, but as with so many other early railroad ideas, nothing materialized. Over the next twenty years, Westminster had its hopes for a railroad connection raised and dashed at least twice more.

Finally, in 1890, the Santa Ana & Westminster Railroad was incorporated by local people for the purpose of building a railroad between those two communities. One of the first tasks of the new company was to obtain permission from the City of Santa Ana to lay a track down the center of one of the town's east-west streets in order to gain access from the west side of town to the established rail depot area on the city's east side. Although promoted as an improvement to the communities it would serve, the railroad's proposed route was not warmly received by those Santa Ana residents whose properties abutted the street the railroad wished to use.

At public hearings held in Santa Ana on the street franchise matter, several Westminster residents appeared to express their desire to have the railroad built, but a number of Santa Ana residents strongly objected, fearing that the value of their homes would be reduced by the railroad's presence. They claimed that the easement belonging to the city in front of their property was for public street purposes only, which did not include the laying of track and the operation of trains. Petitions were filed at subsequent meetings, some citizens praying for approval of the railroad franchise and others asking for denial. The use of horse power rather than steam power was discussed, and alternate routes were hotly argued.

After several months' debate, the franchise for the SA&W right of way was approved by the city in amended form in June 1891. The franchise granted the right to build a track on Second Street for the haulage of freight and passengers, with trains to be drawn or propelled by "street railway-type" locomotives (steam dummies), as nearly smokeless and noiseless as possible, of not more than 20 tons in weight, and to be operated at speeds not to exceed five miles per hour.

Despite these restrictions, there were still several Second Street property owners who opposed the railroad and vowed to block it if work proceeded. The railroad company, however, was committed to building the road as planned, setting the stage for a confrontation. In October 1891, when grading began on Second Street, several property owners agreed to bring legal action at such time as actual tracklaying began across their property. During the month, track materials were received at the Santa Fe depot grounds in preparation for the commencement of construction.

Very early on the morning of November 3, 1891, four or five teams of horses and about 30 men with their grading implements and tools began work. The Superior Court was not yet open at that hour so the first property owner had no way of taking the legal action contemplated to keep the rail crews off his land. As soon as court opened, the next property owner obtained an injunction requiring the railroad to suspend construction across her land. When the sheriff arrived to serve the injunction, he found temporary ties and rails already down and held by a train of work cars. The case was dismissed and the railroad's attorneys advised the men to proceed with their work.

When the foreman in charge of the construction crew gave directions to proceed onto the next piece of property, the landowner began picking up the ties and throwing them back, but he was easily outnumbered and was unable to stop the tracklaying from going forward. When the next piece of property was reached, two young men attempted to stop the horses hauling supplies by grabbing their bridles. And so it went: by noon, several fights had started and been stopped, additional ties and a section of rail laid, and a locomotive run over the completed portion of track. The Superior Court then closed, and the next property owners had no way of keeping the tracklayers off their land. By nightfall, the track had been laid as far as Spurgeon Street, a distance of about a half mile.

In view of this strong negative feeling, and facing several lawsuits filed by angry property owners, the Santa Ana & Westminster's management decided not to proceed any further with the project until the legal questions had been resolved. During the resulting court proceedings, several persons complained that the existence of the railroad had reduced the value of their properties by up to 50 percent, and that there had been little demand for lots on Second Street since the inception of the project. It was further claimed that smoke from passing engines got into houses fronting the railroad — making living conditions unbearable and sometimes causing violent fits of coughing — and that rentals facing the street were difficult to keep occupied because of the dirt and annoyance of the railroad.

The railroad responded that the trains did not, and could not, raise dust at the slow speed at which they were required to run, that trains running at the prescribed five miles per hour made very little noise, and that the slow speed eliminated any danger of anyone being run over. Clearly, both sides were taking extreme positions. Nevertheless, after the cases dragged on for over a year, in December 1892, the court found in favor of the plaintiffs and awarded eight of them nearly $2,000. This verdict was unsatisfactory to the Westminster company since the level of damages awarded effectively obstructed any further extension of the street track towards Westminster. In 1893, the Santa Ana & Newport Railway purchased the Westminster company, whose principal asset was the existing length of track on Second Street. The Newport road used the stub for switching and terminal use in Santa Ana and, in so doing, also assumed as one of its corporate purposes the eventual provision of railroad service to Westminster by whatever route could be built.

This bucolic shelter was the original Shell Beach (Huntington Beach) railway station, built by SA&N's successor Southern Pacific. By the time this circa 1912 photo was taken, these minimal facilities had been eclipsed by the superior Pacific Electric depot near the ocean pier.
– Southern Pacific Transportation Company

This view of a celery field near Smeltzer
was taken about 1900 and shows the
extensive cultivation of that valuable crop
at that time.
– First American Title Insurance
Collection

The Santa Ana & Newport Railway
brought their 2-4-2 tank locomotive No. 2
out of storage to power construction trains
during the building of the Smeltzer
Branch. This 1897 view shows the old
tank engine with a construction train,
probably in Newport.
– Joe Thompson

156

A Branch Line for Celery

The Santa Ana & Newport company was no more successful at negotiating with the remaining, militant Second Street property owners in Santa Ana, so the Westminster extension faded away for awhile. In 1897, the company decided to build toward Westminster from the Newport Beach end of its line. The company was re-incorporated to raise additional capital, and surveyors were placed in the field in July of that year. The line as located ran along the beach from Newport to Shell Beach (later Huntington Beach), and then curved north and ran inland towards Westminster. Conveniently, the right-of-way for the entire extension was acquired in a single grant from the Stearns Rancho Company. The SA&N did its own grading along the beach but engaged the San Bernardino firm of Bright and Crandall (who had participated in the original construction of the SA&N in 1890) to handle the cuts and fills north across the Huntington Beach mesa.

The peatlands through which the Smeltzer branch ran were so unstable that the railroad had to reinforce the subgrade with piles in several areas. Even with this support, there were severe limits to the weight the track structure could accommodate. These limits were apparently exceeded at Smeltzer on this day in 1908, when a 2200-class 4-6-0 rolled over at the height of the celery harvest rush (note the crates piled around the barn in the background). The rescue crane had to approach gingerly from the south.
– Westminster Historical Society

After crossing the mesa the line entered the rich peat land district. Within recent geological time, this low-lying area had formed part of the Santa Ana River's outlet to the sea, and it still was occasionally inundated by overflow waters from the unruly river during periods of very heavy flooding. The rich soil of the district had been formed from the admixture of alluvial silt from the river and decayed vegetable matter from the tule swamps along the river banks. The swampy ground in the peat lands was so soft that the horses used by the railroad builders had to wear special wooden shoes to keep from becoming stuck. So much trouble was experienced in keeping newly laid track from sinking out of sight overnight that piling had to be driven along the line at several points to stabilize the track structure and the sub-grade. In the soft peat ground of D.E. Smeltzer's celery ranch, 10 rail miles from Newport and just a few miles short of their Westminster goal, the 34-man construction crew got as far as they could go. The last rail was laid at 5:25 p.m., October 27, 1897. Although the extension had not quite reached Westminster, the peat lands farming district at last had rail access to the outside world. A crew of 15 men was kept busy for the next month with engine No. 2 — loading and spreading trainloads of gravel ballast in the peat lands to further stabilize the track — while carloads of agricultural products began to be shipped out even before the line was finished.

Domestic celery was the most important item carried out over the new branch. Celery had been introduced into Orange County only a few years earlier by D.E. Smeltzer of St. Louis. A high-value crop, it was also fragile and very perishable, and thus not until the arrival of the railroad could celery become an important crop for Westminster-area farmers. The first cars of celery went out over the SA&N in November 1897, and, on average, about two cars

For a number of years, Smeltzer was the end of the branch line from Newport and Huntington Beach. It was marked by two large barns, one of which is shown here, from which celery was crated and shipped. This 1901 view shows old-style ventilator cars being loaded with the valuable crop.
– Los Angeles County Museum, History Division

were loaded on the branch daily for the next five months. One observer reported "six to ten" cars being loaded in December, and twelve cars were shipped out one day in February at the peak of the celery harvest. The last loads of celery went out in March, and service during the off-season was cut back to just two or three trains a week. Although the real traffic boom had yet to begin, the railroad was already benefitting from its new extension. On February 15, 1898, the Santa Ana & Newport ran an excursion from Santa Ana to the end of the new "Smeltzer Branch" for all who wanted to visit the peat lands. Four hundred participants observed the celery industry, reportedly ate enough of the crop to fill a railroad car, and carried home a week's supply free.

When Senator W. A. Clark and his brother acquired the Santa Ana & Newport Railway in 1899 (see Chapter 3), it was said that he was interested in extending the Smeltzer branch north to his sugar factory at Los Alamitos. Although the factory was already served by the Southern Pacific (see Chapter 1), he apparently hoped to be able to negotiate lower freight rates by having his own railroad carry some of the inbound sugar beets. He also planned to import semi-processed Hawaiian cane sugar (for final processing at his Los Alamitos plant) through the Newport wharf, and to ship finished sugar from the wharf. In the spring of 1899, SA&N surveyors were in the field marking out a route north from Smeltzer. Rights-of-way were actually purchased, and it was reported that the Clark brothers were prepared to spend $75,000 on the railroad. At the same time, however, Southern Pacific surveyors were also noted to be setting grade stakes for a line of their own towards the peat lands, suggesting that if the Clarks persisted in building into territory already served by the Southern Pacific, then the Espee would build into the peat lands and capture traffic away from the SA&N. Senator Clark sent his brother and local representative, J. Ross Clark, to San Francisco to meet with S.P. President Collis Huntington to discuss the situation.

J. Ross Clark returned to Southern California with an agreement which changed the railroad map of Orange County. In exchange for concessions from the S.P. regarding rates to be charged over its existing Los Alamitos Branch to and from the Clarks' sugar factory, the brothers agreed to sell the entire Santa Ana & Newport Railway to the Southern Pacific. As mentioned in Chapter 3, one reason why the Clarks originally purchased the SA&N may have been to secure a tidewater outlet for their proposed railroad from Montana. Subsequently, however, the Federal government decided to improve the harbor facilities at San Pedro. With that seaport now clearly designated as Southern California's primary harbor, Newport declined in strategic value and the Clarks lost interest in the SA&N. (The Clarks then purchased another short line, the Los Angeles Terminal Railway, which gave them access to San Pedro.) The transfer of the Santa Ana & Newport Railway to the Southern Pacific Company was formally announced on June 14, 1899, ending the independent career of Orange County's only successful short line.

Carloadings of celery and other farm products on the line from Newport to Smeltzer continued to grow steadily following its acquisition by the Southern Pacific. By 1903, 2,500 acres of Orange County peat lands were planted with celery, ranking it sixth in area among all county crops, after barley, wheat, hay, beans, beets and corn. By 1906, there were 5,500 acres planted with the product, and the Celery Growers Association of Orange County had 200 members. To give an idea of the railroad traffic which resulted from this crop, one and a half acres yielded 1,200 bunches of celery, which equated to 150 crates or one car load.

Table 5.1
Annual Carloads of Celery
Shipped From Smeltzer Branch Stations
1898-1907

Year Ending in June	Carloads of Celery
1898	300
1899	500
1900	700
1901	1,100
1902	1,200
1903	1,400
1904	1,600
1905	1,800
1906	2,275
1907	1,700

Farms all along the Smeltzer branch north of Huntington Beach contributed to the crop, but the largest carloadings came from Smeltzer and Wintersburg, stations in the heart of the peat lands district. Newland, one mile north of the beach, became an established celery shipping point as late as 1903. The aptly-named station of Celery (located at the foot of what is now Brookhurst at Pacific Coast Highway) was another, more southerly shipping point until it was eliminated in 1905 during the course of a track relocation project between Huntington Beach and Newport.

After the turn of the century, small villages began to form around the railroad stations along the branch where crops were loaded. Typical of these were Smeltzer and Wintersburg. Smeltzer, at the (then) end of the line, was essentially a company town with a lumber warehouse, offices, a small hotel, a blacksmith, a barn capable of holding up to 50 teams of horses, and housing for American and foreign laborers. Wintersburg had a packing shed, a few houses, a church, and an S.P. water tank used to replenish the tenders of locomotives engaged in switching cars of celery during the seasonal rush.

The California Vegetable Union handled the marketing of much of the Orange County celery crop, and their "California Fruit Express" ventilator and refrigerator cars were to be found in great numbers on the Smeltzer branch during the harvest. Most of the crop was washed, trimmed, and crated at the point of shipment, but weighing and icing the cars took place *en route*, after

leaving Orange County. (Some celery was shipped "rough," loaded loose on decks improvised in each rail car, and not finished until it reached midwestern

One of the principal shipping points on the "Huntington Beach Branch" was Wintersburg, about three miles inland from the beach at today's Warner Avenue. At the time of this circa 1912 photo, considerable tonnages of vegetables were shipped out from this station.
– Southern Pacific Transportation Company

Table 5.2
Celery Shipments From
Principal Smeltzer Branch Stations
1905-06

| | Carloads | |
Station	1905	1906
Smeltzer	863	951
Wintersburg	725	717
La Bolsa	14	350
Newland	198	257
Total Carloads	1,800	2,275

distribution points.) At the peak of the harvest season, a second daily train had to be put on to handle all the business offered. This additional train usually ran at night, and was designated by the S.P. as the "Smeltzer Freight." Originating in Los Angeles, the train ran down to Santa Ana at better than twice the speed allowed for other freights over this district, and between Santa Ana and Smeltzer the train was also available to carry passengers. After observing this annual phenomenon, one local newspaper filed this report:

The sleepy old S.P. has woke {sic} up and is sending in a night train to take all the celery away from the peat fields. It looks odd to see the big head light blazing a hole through the banks of gloom and fog at midnight's holy hour! You bet it does. But it is doing it, and the hoarse whistle bellows and the smoke ascends and the weeds are smashed down twice a day on the track instead of once!

On exceptional days, shipments of celery off the Smeltzer branch amounted to more than fifty cars; sometimes two locomotives were required to haul them all. These celery trains had priority over other freight trains all the way to Los Angeles, where they were weighed and iced and put into transcontinental trains destined for Kansas City and eastern points. (The Southern Pacific gained a more direct connection to Kansas City in 1902 when the Chicago, Rock Island & Pacific Railway and the El Paso & South Western Railway completed a line from the Midwest to El Paso via Tucumcari, New Mexico.) Despite this priority handling, these early produce trains were not like the "hotshot reefer blocks" of later years. The journey east averaged less than 20 miles per hour. The train departed Los Angeles in the early morning hours, reaching Indio the first night, Yuma the following morning, Tucson that night, El Paso the next night, not arriving in Kansas City until a full seven days after leaving Orange County! Orange County celery constituted the primary winter supply for the entire country at this time. Florida produced a celery crop from March until June, New York State shipped from June until December, and Orange County supplied the market from November until March.

Sugar Beets

Another farm product which became an important component of Southern Pacific traffic in Orange County was sugar beets. The beet sugar industry began in the United States in 1870, when Ebenezer H. Dyer built the nation's first commercial beet sugar processing factory at Alvarado in Northern California. Western "sugar king" Claus Spreckels got started at Watsonville, California, in 1888. In 1890, the Oxnard brothers, who had sugar interests in New York, Nebraska, San Francisco, and Hawaii, formed what became known as the American Beet Sugar Company and built a 2,000 ton-per-day processing plant at Chino in San Bernardino County. In 1897, the Oxnards built a 900 ton-per-day plant in Ventura County (in what is now the City of Oxnard). That same year Spreckels built a 3,000 ton plant near Salinas and the Clark brothers opened their plant at Los Alamitos in Orange County.

Sugar beet cultivation was introduced into Orange County in the late 1890s, with the first crops being grown primarily in the vicinity of Anaheim and Buena Park. Even prior to the opening of the Los Alamitos plant, beets had become one of the largest volume commodities to be shipped out of the county by rail (2,800 cars out of a total of 9,000 in 1895). Although some of the county's beet production was diverted to the Los Alamitos plant from 1897, a large portion of that traffic continued to move by rail to destinations outside the county.

In 1900, 500 acres of land in Fountain Valley — considered too damp for celery — were planted with sugar beets on an experimental basis. The crop did well and a greater acreage was planted the following year, beginning a major expansion of the planting area from the central county to districts nearer the coast. To handle this new crop, a beet loading station named Newland (for a local farmer) was built in 1903 along the Smeltzer branch on the Huntington Beach mesa. This facility in turn stimulated the planting of yet more acreage in beets, beginning a trend that would continue for another 15 years, particularly in the territory served by this branch line (and later also P.E.'s Santa Ana-Huntington Beach line), as local farmers switched to this high-demand, low-spoilage product. In the first decade of the Twentieth century, rail shipments of sugar beets from Smeltzer branch stations grew steadily, surpassing even celery by 1908.

Table 5.3
Tonnages of Sugar Beets
Shipped From Smeltzer Branch Stations
1904-08

Year	Beets Shipped (Tons)
1904	11,000
1905	21,000
1906	36,000
1907	23,000
1908	41,000

The sugar beet harvest and shipping season ran from mid-summer through October, causing an extension of the period each year during which daily mixed passenger and freight service was offered over the Smeltzer branch. Due to the more frequent trains which crushed the weeds growing between the rails on this branch, one local editor quipped, "the S.P. is doing something these summer days, and the grass grown track [between Smeltzer and Huntington Beach] is beginning to have a seared and yellow look."

Over time this traffic began to take its toll of the lightly-built Newport railway trackage. In January 1906, the night celery train *en route* from Smeltzer to Santa Ana was derailed near Thurin station (near Thurin Street and Newport Avenue in Costa Mesa). Ten cars left the track, plowing it up for several hundred feet; spreading rails were blamed and traffic delayed for 24 hours. In February 1907, cars left the tracks several times, and a wreck almost occurred north of Newport during the third week of the month. On the 26th, two freight cars in the mixed train from Santa Ana derailed two miles north of the

In 1907, Southern Pacific crews built a connecting track from Smeltzer to Stanton, then known as Benedict, on the Los Alamitos Branch, thus completing a loop through Orange County's most productive districts. This picture shows the work train on this project stopped at the site of the future Westminster depot.
— Westminster Historical Society

Another view of the "Benedict cutoff" construction train, pulled by 4-4-0 No. 1383, which remained on SP's roster until 1933, latterly used in movie train service.
— Westminster Historical Society

beach. The climax to this litany of woe came the next day when the mixed train arrived at Newport at noon and attempted to reach Smeltzer with empties. High winds had blown sand over the track along the beach front so the trainmen gave up and tried to back up. Even the retreat proved impossible, however, as a rock on the wye track at "Newport Junction" derailed the locomotive. No wrecker was immediately available and at the end of the day the engine was still stalled in several feet of sand!

When Southern Pacific's track between Newport and Huntington Beach was buried by windblown sand, it could be closed for up to 40 hours while a gang of as many as 100 men worked to sweep and shovel it clear. (This problem also affected the adjacent Pacific Electric line.) The nuisance of blowing sand — plus the deteriorating condition of the lightly-built ex-SA&N tracks — posed a problem for the Southern Pacific. The heavy (albeit seasonal) tonnage of agricultural products which originated on the Smeltzer branch more than offset the demise of traffic to and from the Newport wharf, but the route was roundabout and the trackage generally poor. The S.P. decided to extend the Smeltzer branch northward to a sidetrack station on the Los Alamitos branch called Benedict (now Stanton), both to reduce the amount of running over poor track and to cut substantially overall train mileage.

Southern Pacific crews began grading the northern extension of the Smeltzer branch in 1906, but work was soon interrupted by more important events. In 1905, the Colorado River had broken through its banks and was flowing unchecked into the Imperial Valley, destroying valuable farmland and swamping S.P.'s main line. By mid-1906, the Southern Pacific was mustering

With the completion of S.P.'s "west side" line through Westminster, a standard "No. 23" single story depot was built to serve the community, which had waited twenty years for direct rail service to arrive. There were some complaints, however, about the misspelling of the town's name on the station signboards.
– Southern Pacific Transportation Company

Before World War One, sugar beets became an important Orange County crop. George Carol of Anaheim invented an unloading machine, examples of which were installed at several points along Southern Pacific's trackage. This one at Newland, on the SP near Huntington Beach, looks down the ramp at newly-loaded cars awaiting the arrival of the morning freight train.
— Huntington Beach Junior Chamber of Commerce

construction resources from all over its system to return the river back into the Gulf of California, and no crews or equipment were available for other projects. Not until February 11, 1907, did Espee crews restore the river to its former course, releasing construction forces for other work. Work on the "Smeltzer-Benedict extension" was resumed in the Summer of 1907. From a wye installed at Benedict on the Los Alamitos Branch, the new track inched south. The construction train reached Smeltzer on July 31, 1907, and through trains began operation on August 15th, running from Anaheim to Benedict, Smeltzer and Newport Beach.

During October and November of 1907, a twelve car train was kept busy making four trips each day, hauling gravel to the new Benedict-Smeltzer trackage from a spur located between Huntington Beach and Newport. This point along the beach was later designated "Sandspur" in the S.P. timetable, and became a primary source for sand (used to increase locomotive traction on wet or greasy rail) for Los Angeles Division locomotives. On one of these gravel runs, the tender of the backing locomotive struck a track velocipede — a bicycle-like rail-riding device — a quarter mile north of Weibling station, killing one of the riders who was visiting the telephone operator at Wintersburg. Despite this unfortunate accident, at last the purpose of the 1897 re-incorporation of the SA&N to build to Westminster was achieved, and the promise made by the Clarks to extend the Smeltzer Branch to Los Alamitos fulfilled.

The Benedict-Smeltzer extension was completed by the construction of a depot, section house, water tank, side track and beet dump at Westminster. This station in the heart of the fertile peat lands originated a substantial

166

This view of a Carol beet loader in action, filling a car of SP-affiliate Morgan's Louisiana & Texas Railway, was taken at Stanton, circa 1914.
– First American Title Company

portion of the extensive agricultural traffic carried by Espee in western Orange County.

With the opening of the new trackage, S.P.'s local train services were re-routed. The former off-season tri-weekly train schedule was superseded by a year-round daily except Sunday accommodation train (mixed passenger and freight) effective September 1, 1907. This new service functioned as a "mixed train to everywhere," and was an outgrowth of the old "Los Alamitos & Tustin Passenger & Freight" of earlier years (which had been extended to Newport and Smeltzer following S.P.'s acquisition of the SA&N). The new mixed train began at Los Alamitos in the morning, running east to Anaheim, and making a round trip out to Tustin and back to Anaheim. It then went south to Santa Ana and Newport, up the old SA&N line to Huntington Beach and Smeltzer, continuing on to Westminster, Benedict, and Anaheim before returning west to Los Alamitos for the night.

For a single month after the opening of "the loop" in 1907, Southern Pacific supplemented this "mixed train to everywhere" with two faster passenger trains operating over the same circuit of track, one operating clockwise around the loop in the morning, the other counter-clockwise in the evening. Apparently there was insufficient patronage to support such a lavish schedule and these two passenger trains were deleted from the timetable issued October 1, 1907, making them among the shortest-lived trains in Orange County history.

After a few months of operation, the "mixed train to everywhere" was altered to begin and end its daily run in Santa Ana instead of Los Alamitos. For sixteen years this single daily one-way mixed train — known to local Espee employees as "the Merry-go-round" — was an Orange County institution, traversing virtually all Southern Pacific trackage in Orange County.

As farmers began to appreciate the contractual security of raising beets compared to the uncertainties of other crops, acreage devoted to beets in Orange County increased from 4,000 acres in 1903 to 27,000 in 1912. A typical yield was 10 tons per acre, which translated to big tonnages for the serving railroads, primarily the Southern Pacific and the Pacific Electric. This huge volume could be speedily loaded thanks to a man named George Carrol who invented a facility for transferring beets from field wagons to railroad cars. Carrol's "Patent Dump" consisted of ramps and a mechanism for tipping the wagons so their contents could be dumped into the rail cars below. (Mr. Carrol's home, now a private school, still stands near the S.P. Anaheim station.)

Eventually beet dumps were built at nearly every sidetrack station on Espee's North Orange County lines. Important dumps were at Newland, La Bolsa, Wintersburg (3), Smeltzer (2), Sugar, Westminster, Stanton, Anaheim, Buena Park, and South Santa Ana. These were supplemented by additional dumps at points in the Fountain Valley area along Pacific Electric's Santa Ana to Huntington Beach line, built in 1909 (see Chapter 4). The average dump could load from 10 to 15 railroad cars on a peak day during the harvest season; some facilities could handle even more. During the beet harvest, it was a common sight during early morning hours to see all the waiting railroad cars filled and a dozen or so eight-mule teams waiting for the morning freight to bring more empty cars.

Railroad involvement with Orange County's sugar beet industry did not end with the transportation of the raw material from the fields. The construction of four new processing plants in Orange County between 1909 and 1912 meant that the serving railroads also carried fuels, bags of processed sugar, and various by-products to and from the factories. All these facilities were heavily rail-oriented, with elaborate track layouts to facilitate the unloading of beets, intra-plant movements, and the shipment of finished sugar. Each of the factories had a main building four or five stories high, and all were imposing fixtures on the central Orange County plain otherwise devoid of much heavy industry at that time.

With the construction of these new sugar beet processing plants in Orange County, the stage was set for a period of extensive cultivation of the profitable crop. A significant amount of arable land was devoted to growing sugar beets during the 1910s, and one might imagine that, with factories so close to the fields, short haul rail-borne beet traffic would have declined. In fact the opposite was true: this period saw the county's railroad network carry an intensive sugar-related traffic. Many local growers contracted to sell their beet crop to more distant processors (notably at Chino and Oxnard) and a considerable proportion of the beets processed in Orange County factories was shipped in from points outside the county (generally from Los Angeles and San Diego Counties). Further, except in the case of very short hauls, rail cars were the best way to handle the huge volume of the beet crop, so short hauls within the county continued to be handled by the railroads as well.

Many of these movements involved hauling by more than one carrier; the Santa Fe, to give one example, would carry loaded cars up from the beet growing district around Fallbrook, transfer the loads at Santa Ana to the S.P., who would in turn hand the loads over to the Pacific Electric at Dyer for delivery to the plant at Delhi. Another common pattern was for the P.E. to bring solid train loads of beets into the county down the Newport line from Dominguez and turn the train over to the S.P. at Newport; S.P. crews had to back the train onto the old ocean wharf (little used by this time) to gain enough momentum to pull the heavy train up the stiff, 1.2 percent grade toward Santa Ana. Besides the beets, other materials moved included chemicals used in the processing (mainly lime and bone charcoal), bags for packaging, coal and oil fuel for the factory boilers, and finished sugar and molasses. Waste beet pulp was also used as cattle feed and there was a significant movement of this by-product to cattle feed lots elsewhere (as well as cattle to corrals near the factories). Given the intensity and volume of the operations, it seems appropriate that the annual beet harvesting and processing rush was likened to a military operation by being designated a "campaign."

The five sugar factories in Orange County accounted for over 25 percent of all beet sugar output in the state at this time and represented nearly 20 percent of the nation's entire output. By 1912 beets and beet sugar had become

The Southern California Sugar Company built a plant at Delhi, south of Santa Ana, in 1909. This facility was served by Pacific Electric, whose Santa Ana-Huntington Beach main line may be seen crossing South Main Street in this circa 1912 photo.
– First American Title Company

SPENCE
Air Photos

In response to the increasing local cultivation of sugar beets, several beet sugar processing factories were built in Orange County around the turn of the century. Holly Sugar Company built this plant at La Bolsa, north of Huntington Beach, in 1911. The Southern Pacific branch runs from upper left to middle right in this early 1920s aerial view.

– Spence Air Photos

Orange County's most valuable agricultural product; that year's beet crop was valued at $3.5 million and the refined sugar at $5 million, compared to $2.5 million for oranges, $1.8 million for beans, and a total of $26 million for all agricultural production in the county. Acreage devoted to the beet crop climbed during the 1910s, peaking at 50,000 acres in 1917. At Huntington Beach and La Bolsa alone, Southern Pacific and Pacific Electric together handled 100,000 tons of sugar-related traffic for the year 1916. During the "campaign," sometimes as many as 200 cars would be carried on a single day, extra clerks were put on to keep track of the business, and extra switching and train crews were needed to keep traffic moving. In 1918 S.P. opened a depot at La Bolsa housed in an old boxcar, thus ending five years of representation by the P.E. agent at nearby Huntington Beach.

This intensive seasonal traffic was not without incident, especially as much of the traffic moved over poorly-built branch lines. In August of 1915 there was a wreck at Westfall — a siding just south of La Bolsa — when three cars of beets left the track at a switch. Beets and pieces of wrecked cars were

170

An SP diesel pulls a long string of empty sugar beet gondolas past the Southern Pacific Santa Ana depot in the late 1950s. The cars have come from the beet sugar factory at Dyer, a couple of miles to the south.
— Tom Gildersleeve

Southern Pacific No. 1404 delivers a trainload of sugar beets to the Holly Sugar plant at Dyer, July 1957.
— Southern Pacific photo by A.W. Rommel, William A. Myers Collection

Table 5.4
Orange County Sugar Beet Factories
1897-1914

Factory Location	Year Built	Building Company	Slicing Capacity (tons/day)	Shipments (100 lb. bags/year)	Serving Railroad
Los Alamitos	1897	Alamitos Sugar Co.	800	155,000	SP
Delhi	1909	So. Calif. Sugar Co.	600	146,000	SP & PE
Anaheim	1911	Anaheim Sugar Co.	800	150,000	AT&SF
La Bolsa	1911	Holly Sugar Co.	750	150,000	SP & PE
Dyer	1912	Santa Ana Co-op.	600	192,000	SP & PE

This view of the Los Alamitos sugar plant was taken in the summer of 1924, when the factory's power plant was leased to Southern California Edison during a regional power shortage.
– Photo by G. Haven Bishop, Southern California Edison Company Historical Collection

Notes:

Annual shipments of finished sugar are given in 100-pound bags; a 150,000 bag plant shipped roughly 600 to 700 (25 ton) railroad cars each year.

The La Bolsa plant was expanded in 1912 to a daily beet slicing capacity of 1,400 tons, with a resulting shipping capacity of 326,000 bags annually.

The Dyer plant was expanded in 1914 to a daily beet slicing capacity of 1,200 tons.

Expansion at other plants brought the total Orange County processing capacity to 5,900 tons of beets annually by 1917.

Pacific Electric access to the La Bolsa factory was via trackage rights over S.P.'s Smeltzer Branch (see Chapter 4).

Another beet sugar factory was built by the Santa Ana Cooperative at Dyer, and was served by both Southern Pacific and Pacific Electric. A careful look at this mid-1920s aerial view reveals overhead catenary (electric trolley wires) on most rail spurs in this plant.
– Santa Ana Public Library

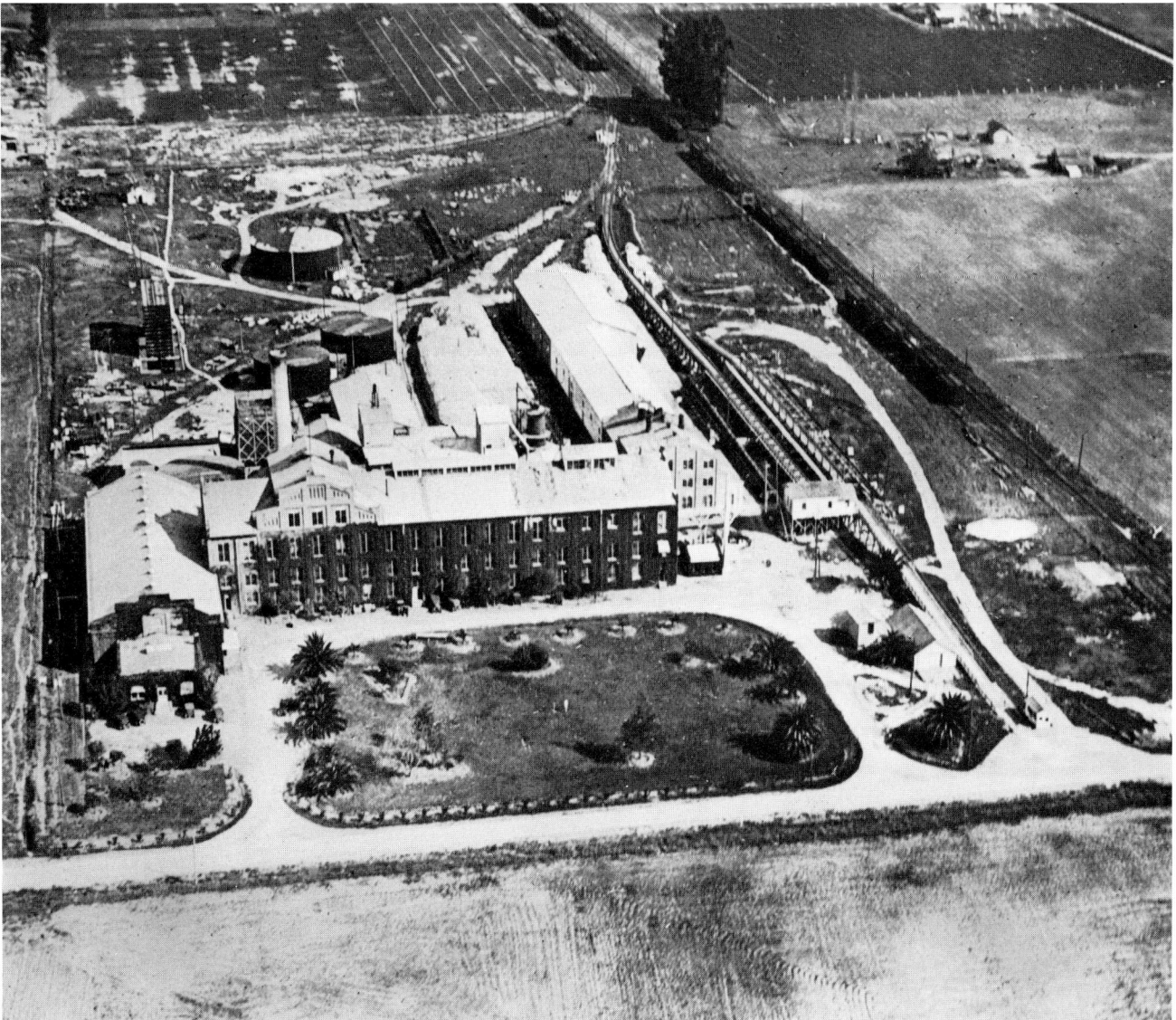

Heavy freight movements into and around Orange County were often handled by 4-8-0 "Twelve Wheelers," such as Southern Pacific No. 2922, seen here at Santa Ana on June 12, 1924.
— R.P. Middlebrook photo, Arnold Menke Collection

Santa Fe Consolidation No. 1988 was captured on film as it switched the packing houses at Irvine depot in 1924.
— R.P. Middlebrook photo, Stan Kistler Collection

scattered, the track was torn up and poles broken down (this section of S.P. track was jointly operated with the Pacific Electric at this time, see Chapter 4), and flanges were even broken off some of the car wheels. Despite the magnitude of the mess, however, it was quickly cleaned up and traffic returned to normal.

Sugar beet and other rail operations were even more severely impacted by the heavy rains and flooding of 1916 which washed out bridges and tracks in Orange County. Both the Pacific Electric and Southern Pacific (ex-SA&N) tracks between Huntington Beach and Newport were washed out by the rampaging Santa Ana River. Although the P.E. soon repaired its line the S.P.

Santa Fe's ubiquitous Nineteen-hundred class Consolidations were commonly used in freight service in Orange County during the steam era. No. 1975 was seen at Santa Ana in 1925.
– R.P. Middlebrook photo, Stan Kistler Collection

tracks were not restored until 1918; during the intervening years S.P. trains could not travel directly between the two beach cities. Because this broke S.P.'s circle of branch lines in the west county, trains destined to either Newport or Huntington Beach were forced to turn back after coming down to each point from the interior. (Despite this, the "Merry-go-round" train continued to appear on operating timetables until 1923.)

Sugar beet traffic climaxed in Orange County during 1916 and 1917 and then began to decline due to crop disease and deteriorating economics (primarily because of the relaxation of sugar import tariffs, and the increase in production of cane sugar in Hawaii and Louisiana). This decline resulted in consolidations among the manufacturing companies followed by a contraction of processing and rail operations. Holly Sugar, which owned the La Bolsa factory, acquired the Santa Ana Co-operative Sugar Company, which owned the plant at Dyer, in 1917. Holly already owned the Delhi factory through its subsidiary, the Southern California Sugar Company, and further acquired the Anaheim plant in 1923. In that year both the Delhi and Anaheim plants were closed and dismantled, with remaining production being concentrated at Dyer and La Bolsa. In 1926 the Alamitos Sugar Company closed its outmoded Los Alamitos plant and came to an agreement with Holly to operate the Dyer facility jointly. That same year Holly dismantled its La Bolsa plant and moved it to Wyoming, leaving the Dyer plant as the sole survivor. Holly's Dyer plant proved to be a hardy survivor, remaining in production through the 1970s, although by that time running on beets brought in from the Imperial Valley by the Southern Pacific.

An Agricultural Miscellany

The main product which replaced sugar beets in the west county after World War One was lima beans. Even though bean warehouses and loading stations were established along the railroads (primarily at Buena Park and Smeltzer on the Southern Pacific, at Greenville and Garden Grove on the Pacific Electric, and at Irvine and El Toro on the Santa Fe), this crop never approached the volume of the former sugar beet harvests, or the complexity.

While vegetables and field crops proliferated on the coastal plain of western Orange County, and grain and beans covered most of the southeastern valleys, nuts and fruit became the predominant crops grown in the interior and

During the steam era, SP assigned two or three engines to handle Orange County's freight traffic. Typical of the power used was Mogul (2-6-0) No. 1765, seen here in front of the Santa Ana depot about 1950. This locomotive is now preserved at the Lomita Railroad Museum.
– Marshall Nelson

The decline of steam power after World War Two brought some unusual locomotives into Orange County. Bumped from passenger service, high-drivered Pacific (4-6-2), Southern Pacific No. 2447 ran out its flue time in perishible freight service, and is seen in Santa Ana about 1950.
– Marshall Nelson

upland portions of the county. At the turn of the century apricots were grown in some quantity and shipped (in dried form) primarily from stations along the Southern Pacific's Tustin Branch. Production of this deciduous fruit peaked about 1909, when there were 160,000 trees bearing some 9,000 tons of fruit annually. It should be added that after drying, the shipping weight of the crop declined to about a fourth of the harvest weight.

Walnuts succeeded apricots in importance during the 1910s. Nine thousand tons were harvested from 300,000 trees in 1919. Walnut packing houses were established on railroad spurs at La Habra, Fullerton, Anaheim, Orange, Santa Ana, Irvine and Capistrano, and shipments from each of these facilities averaged a hundred car loads annually, bringing as much as $3 million in receipts to the growers. These crops notwithstanding, the tree that ultimately covered the greatest acreage, filled the most railroad cars, and provided the greatest income was the Valencia orange.

Railroads and the Citrus Industry in Orange County

Oranges, most notably the Valencia type, were first successfully grown in Southern California in the late 1870s, primarily in the dry, interior San Gabriel and Riverside-San Bernardino Valleys. Citrus made its appearance in the Santa Ana Valley by the 1880s. Although the cultivation of oranges got off to a more gradual start in Orange County than in neighboring Los Angeles, Riverside and San Bernardino Counties, they were grown in sufficient quantity to make the name of the new county appropriate when it was formed in 1889.

Despite this, Southern California citrus production was comparatively small — and local in distribution — until several developments occurred.

In later years, Santa Fe Pacifics were sometimes used to wheel "citrus blocks" out of the county on the first leg of their transcontinental journeys. No. 1226 was at Santa Ana in 1941.
– R.P. Middlebrook photo, Stan Kistler Collection

First, a mass market had to be created for citrus fruit, which in the late
nineteenth century was widely perceived to be a luxury item. The development
of such markets around the nation largely depended upon the railroad
industry's ability to ship citrus promptly and inexpensively. This in turn
required improvements in technology to permit faster transcontinental train
schedules and to perfect special cars capable of carrying the perishible fruit
with a minimum of spoilage.

Improvements in motive power, track, and signalling technology at the
turn of the century enabled the transcontinental railroads serving Southern
California to speed up their train services. This speed up was enhanced by
competition, especially between the Southern Pacific and the Santa Fe, as each
carrier learned that speed was the key to capturing the bulk of perishable
shipments from Southern California fields.

Concurrently came the perfecting of ventilated (and then insulated and
refrigerated) railroad cars which could protect the perishable cargo from
temperature extremes, thus retaining the fruit's freshness during the long haul
across the continent. Although ventilated fruit cars appeared on western
railroads in the 1880s, they were not manufactured in great quantity, and were
not reliable in operation, until after the turn of the century.

The cost of refrigeration had to be reduced as well. Railroad refrigerator cars required prodigious amounts of ice (until the introduction of mechanical refrigeration units in the 1950s). Southern California's mild winters meant that natural ice could not be harvested and stored for use during the fruit shipping season; instead, local ice supplies were manufactured in refrigeration plants. Until the late 1890s, when cheaper hydroelectric power began to supplant costly steam engines as prime movers in the refrigeration plants, the expense of manufacturing the ice often made the cost of shipping California citrus prohibitive. This was especially true in Orange County where hydroelectric energy was not available until 1899, and then only in Fullerton, Orange and Santa Ana. (This may be one reason why no major railroad icing plants were ever built in Orange County.)

Finally, once these technological improvements had been made, a national market established for citrus, and additional acreage planted to meet the increased demand, it took as many as ten years for the young trees to mature to

(Overleaf) In the first decade of the Twentieth Century, citrus acreage increased as north Orange County ranchers were attracted to the potential profits of these high-value fruits. This view of Yorba Linda about 1915 shows the extensive citrus groves surrounding the tiny commercial core of the community, and the two large packing houses (right of center) that were served by the Pacific Electric Railway. The P.E. Depot is at the far left. – Cochem and Ron Sands (Historical Panoramics of Orange County)

179

No58.

the point where they produced a marketable crop. Although initial planting of citrus began in the county in the 1880s, substantial increases in acreage were not made until the late 1910s and again in the 1930s. Orange County had 40,000 acres dedicated to citrus by 1920 and 75,000 acres by 1940.

Rail shipments of Orange County oranges began in the 1880s, growing from under 100 to over 300 carloads annually during that decade. In the 1890s shipments rose to 1,000 carloads annually, originating from Santa Ana, Anaheim, Tustin and Orange. Increases in citrus acreage after the turn of the century resulted in corresponding boosts in harvests and railroad shipments (five acres of orange trees yielded an average of one carload of fruit each year).

By the mid-1920s, despite its small size, Orange County ranked as the leading producer of Valencia oranges in the state. The orchards marched in neat rows across Orange County, manicured forests of millions of trees, abutting all of the county's inland cities and most of its rail lines.

Not only did this acreage of orchards create a lush environment, it resulted in a freight bonanza for the county's railroads. The phenomenal growth of citrus production in Orange County in the Twentieth Century is shown in Table 5.5. The volumes represent all marketable oranges, lemons and grapefruit harvested in the county. While in the 1920s nearly the entire crop was shipped by rail fresh to the east, in ensuing decades a growing proportion was reduced to juice by local processors (10% in the 1930s; 20% in the 1940s; and 30% in the 1950s) before being shipped to market.

Table 5.5
Orange County Citrus Production
1900-1960

| Year | Acres | Trees | Harvests | |
			Boxes	Tons
1900	6,000	360,000	900,000	25,000
1910	8,750	525,000	1,322,000	46,270
1915	13,200	838,000	2,000,000	66,417
1920	40,025	2,449,000	3,976,000	139,160
1925	50,269	2,865,000	5,160,000	361,200
1930	61,516	3,321,000	12,680,000	443,800
1940	75,405	5,435,000	13,157,000	460,498
1945	77,036	5,561,000	20,917,000	545,845
1950	65,684	5,842,000	18,616,000	485,798
1955	54,283	4,120,000	11,535,000	302,668
1960	40,000	3,129,000	12,466,000	327,098

Source: U.S. Bureau of the Census and Department of Agriculture

Packing house prices varied from two to four dollars per box in the 1920s, then dropped to between one and two dollars from the early 1930s through the early 1950s, with a brief upswing to three dollars a box during the mid-1940s. Orange County's 1914 citrus crop was worth $2.9 million; that of 1940 $12.7 million. The $46.2 million value of 1945's crop was the all-time high; by 1950 the crop had retreated in value to only $20 million. The railroads benefitted greatly from this traffic, often earning as much as the growers (up to $1.00 per box) in the process of hauling the fruit to market across the country.

Pacific Electric's diminutive gas-mechanical switcher No. 1647 operated on the isolated and non-electrified "Marlboro island" trackage north of Orange. Here it is shunting a PFE (Pacific Fruit Express) refrigerator car on the grounds of the Orange depot, circa 1951.
– Marshall Nelson

Pacific Electric gas electric locomotive No. 1649, rebuilt from a Brill rail car, was also regularly found on the Orange "island" trackage in the late 1930s.
– R.P. Middlebrook photo, Stan Kistler Collectiion

In the early years citrus was packed at the freight depots owned by the railroads and some of those depots eventually were devoted exclusively to that function. As the traffic grew, however, large, specialized packing houses were built alongside the railroads, often by the co-operative shipping associations which assumed an increasing responsibility for the marketing of the crop. By the early 1920s there were 31 citrus packing houses located along the county's rail lines in the "citrus belt" at La Habra (2), Fullerton (5), Anaheim (4), Santa Ana (3), Tustin (3), Orange (2), Villa Park (2), Yorba Linda (2), Olive (2), Garden Grove, El Modena, McPherson, Brea, Irvine, and Placentia (on the "cut-off" line built by the Santa Fe in 1910). At these facilities the fruit collected from the orchards was washed, graded, wrapped, crated, cooled, and

Villa Park on S.P.'s Tustin Branch remained a sizeable shipping point for citrus into the 1970s. This December 1961 view shows a Baldwin-built diesel pulling a lone refrigerator car westbound from the packing house. The open roof hatches indicate that the car has not yet been iced.
— Ed Workman

CF7 No. 2523 is seen switching cars at the Irvine Valencia Association's packing house at Kathryn on the Venta Spur, circa 1978.
— C.R. Prather

loaded aboard the waiting "reefer cars" set out on adjacent tracks. Each packing house could process from several hundred up to two thousand carloads per season; some were even served by more than one railroad.

This agri-business was very important to the railroads and even spurred some new line construction in Orange County. In 1917 Pacific Electric completed a new line from Laon Junction (just east of La Habra on the Yorba

Agricultural produce from the vast Irvine Ranch was still shipped by rail into the late 1970s. Santa Fe CF7 No. 2550 is seen crossing the Venta Spur bridge over Interstate 5 about 1979. Road switchers like this were often stationed at Santa Ana or Fullerton but could come all the way from San Bernardino if traffic warrented.
– C.R. Prather

Growing urban sprawl would soon engulf this bucolic, late 1970s scene of fields and eucalyptus wind breaks at Myford on the Venta Spur.
– C.R. Prather

186

CF7 No. 2524 and a short train of mechanical refrigerator cars at the curve at Browning on the Venta Spur, circa 1978.
– C.R. Prather

Linda line) to Fullerton (see Chapter 4). This new electric line ran for five miles through the rolling hills of the Bastanchury Ranch which was to develop one of the largest citrus orchards in the world. By 1921 the P.E. had built up a big business on its north Orange County lines amounting to 2,000 carloads from six packing houses. In 1923, over the unsuccessful protests of the electric line, the Union Pacific opened an extension into this district (see page 191) following a route which largely paralleled the existing P.E. tracks. During this same time the Santa Fe built a long spur of its own to reach the shipping facilities on the Bastanchury Ranch. Further south, the Santa Fe constructed what eventually became the five-mile long Venta Spur to reach packing houses in Tustin and on the Irvine Ranch. (Even after Orange County citrus acreage had peaked as a whole the Irvine Ranch continued to expand its groves, devoting more than 5,000 acres to the fruit during the 1950s.)

By the 1940s, the number of packing houses in Orange County had risen to forty-five and the harvest "campaigns" had become a complex pattern of rail movements painstakingly orchestrated by the railroads. During the harvest season, which ran primarily from April to November, all four railroad companies brought a steady procession of empty refrigerator cars into the county to be spotted at the packing houses. Loaded cars were carried to assembly points outside the county to be iced, blocked (assembled into groups of cars destined for specific delivery points), and forwarded eastward in solid trainloads with other market-bound California citrus. The railroads established entire departments (e.g., the Santa Fe Refrigerator Department) or subsidiary companies (S.P. and U.P.'s jointly-owned Pacific Fruit Express, which also serviced the Pacific Electric) to handle this traffic. These agencies managed car construction and maintenance, dispatching, diversion (the ability to enable shippers to divert to different destinations cars already *en route* in order to take advantage of changing market conditions), and refrigeration services. They also worked with the various "exchanges" (often united under a well publicized

187

brand name, such as "Sunkist" or "Mutual") to develop optimum shipping practices and to promote the growers' production.

In addition to the fruit itself, the railroads also carried a substantial "inbound" traffic in citrus-related items. Crating material, or "shook", usually amounted to one carload for every ten cars of fruit. Barrels of smudge pot oil were an important item during the winter months and often received priority handling when frost threatened. Ice had to be shipped from the big regional ice plants to those locations without refrigeration. (There were no railroad ice plants in Orange County; the Santa Fe operated a big facility in San Bernardino, and Pacific Fruit Express had icing plants at S.P.'s Taylor Yard in Los Angeles, at Walnut [City of Industry], and at Colton, all of which were used by the S.P., U.P., and P.E.)

To handle all this business the railroads put on extra crews and trains and the men worked long hours to move the crop in an orderly fashion. The Pacific Electric doubled up on freight service during the rush. Its heaviest traffic was on the La Habra-Yorba Linda line. The Southern Pacific also added freight crew assignments during the harvest rush. P.E. and S.P. citrus carloads were concentrated at Taylor Yard; most was forwarded to Colton for blocking and shipment east, but a smaller percentage was shipped north over the San Joaquin Valley route. The Union Pacific, whose line into Orange County was built in the early 1920s primarily to tap this lucrative traffic, had to be content with the smallest share. During the county's harvest rush extra freights were dispatched daily by both the S.P. and U.P. on an "as needed" basis from the big Pacific Fruit Express facility in Walnut (now City of Industry).

The Santa Fe handled the lion's share of the crop; by the 1940s this amounted to over 12,000 carloads of Orange County citrus annually. The traffic was so great that the railroad established a regular "dedicated traffic" switching crew during the months of the citrus harvest. Based in Santa Ana, the crew worked the Irvine area in the afternoon, Orange and Anaheim at night, and sometimes the crew went as far afield as Olive and Fullerton. This crew routinely handled up to forty cars daily and often put in the then-statutory limit of twelve hours on the road. In addition to this purpose-dedicated switch crew, Santa Fe's local freights from Los Angeles and San Bernardino would work the citrus plants, and the "pick up" and through freights passing through the county would also pick up or drop off cars as needed. Each night the Santa Fe would also run one or two "citrus turns" into Orange County, bringing in solid strings of empty refrigerator cars from San Bernardino, doing switching work at some packing houses, and returning loaded cars to San Bernardino, the marshalling point for eastward-bound produce travelling over Santa Fe lines.

Orange County's rail-borne citrus traffic peaked in 1945 but remained strong into the 1960s before succumbing to spreading urbanization. Rail shipments of citrus and citrus products subsequently diminished as remaining growers and marketers shifted to motor truck carriers in the 1970s. During the seven decades it lasted, however, the steady stream of refrigerated fruit provided abundant testimony that the county had, indeed, been aptly named.

The only known photograph of regular passenger service on Union Pacific's Anaheim Branch is this view of a McKeen car at Fullerton in 1923.
– Union Pacific, John Signor Collection

6000-class Consolidations were common motive power on Union Pacific branch lines. Here 2-8-0 No. 6085 takes a spin on the company's turntable at the end of the Orange County Branch at Anaheim, about 1950.
– James Witaker

Union Pacific's Anaheim Branch

Union Pacific was the last major transcontinental to build into Orange County and it was the county's citrus traffic which attracted the railroad's notice. Since the 1880s the Union Pacific had hoped to build a line from Utah to Southern California but the project was repeatedly delayed. At the turn of the century William Andrews Clark planned his own railroad from Butte, Montana, to Salt Lake City and Los Angeles and purchased two Southern California short lines to further this project (see page 92).

Ultimately Clark and the Union Pacific consolidated their interests, each holding a half-interest in the San Pedro, Los Angeles and Salt Lake Railroad (renamed the Los Angeles and Salt Lake Railroad in 1916) locally called the

"Salt Lake Route." Construction of the line between Salt Lake City and Los Angeles was completed in 1910. Initially this new transcontinental route to Southern California was not heavily promoted by the Union Pacific System which also controlled the Southern Pacific at the time. This attitude changed after December 2, 1912, when the U.S. Supreme Court ordered Union Pacific to relinquish control of the Southern Pacific. Thereafter the Salt Lake Route took on new importance.

Attracted by the growing citrus traffic originating in Orange County, the Salt Lake's managers decided to build a branch line into the citrus belt in the northern part of the county. By this time regulation of the rail industry at both the state and Federal levels was effective enough to mute the type of opposition from railroads already serving the district as had been experienced a decade earlier by the Pacific Electric.

During 1916 the Salt Lake Route announced it intended to build a branch from Pico (Whittier Junction) to Whittier. This action was ratified by the California Railroad Commission in December of that year in the form of an authorization to construct grade crossings. (The Interstate Commerce Commission did not assume regulatory authority over line construction until the passage of the Transportation Act of 1920.) In its application the Salt Lake Route referred to the proposed extension as "practically a spur track" and there was no mention of any intention to build into Orange County.

Shortly after, the intent of the Salt Lake Route was revealed when it applied to the State Commission for authority to issue bonds to cover certain capital expenses. One of the items was $338,503.18 for "the cost of constructing the Santa Ana Branch from Santa Ana to Pico" (of which slightly more than $320,000 represented the cost of purchasing right of way for the proposed 24-mile branch). The Commission approved the bond issue (and thus the project) on April 30, 1917.

In August the State Commission approved the Salt Lake Route's application to construct grade crossings over highways and other railroads in order to extend its branch line from Whittier to Fullerton. Despite this approval, and although most of the right of way had been acquired, the extension was not built at this time due to the entry of the United States into World War I. Even before the Federal Government took control of the steam railroads on December 26, 1917, shortages of manpower and materials forced the Salt Lake Route to delay construction of the extension to Fullerton.

The period of Federal control ended on March 1, 1920. A year later the Salt Lake Route filed an application with the state commission asking for permission to extend its authorized (but not yet built) line south from Fullerton to Anaheim. This was granted; at the same time the railroad obtained a franchise from the City of Anaheim. By early 1922 it appeared that at last the Union Pacific would build into Orange County.

Then the City of Fullerton intervened to protest the routing of the proposed extension. The 1917 route would have had the Salt Lake Route tracks pass through Fullerton's business district parallel to, but a quarter mile south of, the existing Santa Fe line. The city expressed concern over the numerous grade crossings on the new railway line, especially the crossing of South Spadra Road (now Harbor Boulevard) which was at that time a state highway carrying a heavy volume of motor traffic. During 1922 Fullerton sought to have the U.P. compelled to run over the Santa Fe tracks through town and to have a grade separation built over South Spadra Road. Not until the end of the year was a compromise finally reached. Under its terms the Union Pacific agreed to lay its tracks on a right of way adjacent to the south side of the Santa Fe's property. The Santa Fe agreed to permit the U.P. to cross its tracks at grade in west Fullerton (Basta Tower later controlled this interlocking plant). The city agreed to permit grade level crossings of its streets and the Santa Fe and U.P. jointly agreed to fund the installation and maintenance of "automatic flagmen" (wig-wag type warnings) at all crossings except West Commonwealth (now Commonwealth Avenue) and South Spadra Road, each of which received crossing gates. With this last hurdle cleared the Union Pacific hastened to build its branch line into Orange County.

Although the extension continued to be referred to as the "Santa Ana Branch" until construction actually began, U.P.'s franchise from the City of Anaheim ended just south of South Street, well short of Santa Ana. Although some right of way was secured south of that point, the U.P. never built south of Anaheim.

Construction work on Union Pacific's new Anaheim Branch began early in 1923 and was pushed at a rapid pace. The line opened for passenger service on Sunday, July 1, 1923, even though the depots at Fullerton and Anaheim were incomplete (both were finished within 30 days). The first day was tragically eventful as the first northbound train struck an automobile at Hadley Street in Whittier, killing four persons.

Union Pacific offered two "motor trains" over the branch each day, using McKeen "windsplitter" cars. The morning round trip left Central Station in Los Angeles at 8:45 a.m., returning at 11:23 a.m.; the afternoon round trip left Los Angeles at 1:55 p.m. and returned at 4:25 p.m. By this time the famous McKeen design was nearing the end of its lifespan; this was the last new passenger service to be started in Southern California using McKeens. Ironically, just a month after the start of U.P.'s passenger service, rival Southern Pacific discontinued its two daily McKeen "motor trains" to Anaheim.

The total cost of the 18-mile branch was just over $2 million, of which $988,000 was for right of way purchases and $44,000 was for two citrus packing houses (in Anaheim and La Habra). This latter expense was of concern to all of the railroads in Orange County who were often expected to foot the bill for the construction of on-line packing houses. In the mid-Twenties (certainly by 1926) the railroad companies had agreed among themselves to refuse to fund further packing house construction and this expense shifted to the growers' associations.

(Pages 192-195) Excerpts from Southern Pacific Company, Los Angeles Division Timetable, September 1, 1910.
– Bob Kern Collection

Length of Sidings in feet, and location of Scales, Fuel, Water and Turning Stations.						**SECOND CLASS** 110 Santa Ana Freight Leave Daily Ex. Sunday	152 San Pedro Freight Leave Daily Ex. Sunday	276 Mixed Leave Daily Ex. Sunday		108 Santa Ana Passenger Leave Daily	Lo F Lea
16,813 YWTOF						10.25 PM	10.00 PM			5.20 PM	
1,498						10.40	10.20			5.29	
I											
1,382						10.55	10.25			5.31	
5,984 IYWP						11.20	10.40 PM			▪ 5.34	▪
1,164											
I											
1,422						11.30				f 5.39	
764										f	
1,277						11.55				▪ 5.46	
2,296 P						12.10 AM 1.30				▪ 5.52	
2,054						1.55				▪ 5.57	
1,198						2.05				f 6.01	
5,782						2.30				▪X6.08	
1,260						2.35				6.10	
990						2.45				f 6.13	
3,560 WY						3.05				▪ **6.18**	
3,560 WY											
1,635											
3,560						3.05				**6.18**	
6,146						3.25				▪ 6.22	
						3.35		2.10 PM		▪ 6.26	
						4.00		2.15		6.28	
1,195						4.15		f 2.25		f 6.31	
12,008 WYTFP						6.00 AM		3.00 PM		6.40 PM	
528											
661											
1,108											
5,158 WY											
						Arrive Daily Ex.Monday	Arrive Daily Ex. Sunday	Arrive Daily Ex. Sunday		Arrive Daily	Ar

7.35)   (0.40)   (0.50   (1 20)
4.44   8.10   6.12   24.96

Westward trains are superior to trains of the same class in the opposite direction

DIVISION

TIME TABLE
No. 107
September 1, 1910

FIRST CLASS

20 Whittier Passenger — Daily Ex. Sunday	274 Mixed — Leave Wednesday Only	272 Mixed — Leave Daily Ex. Sunday and Wed.	392 Fernando and Santa Ana Motor — Leave Daily	140 San Pedro Passenger — Leave Daily	102 Newport Beach Passenger — Leave Daily	270 Mixed — Leave Daily Ex. Sunday	394 San Pedro Motor — Leave Daily	Distance from San Francisco	STATIONS
.00 PM			10.40 AM	9.05 AM	8.55 AM		4.00 AM	484.7	Aut. Sigs. DN-R **LOS ANGELES** — 2.7
.09			10.49	9.14	9.04		4.09	487.4	VERNONDALE — 0.9
								488.3	Crossing A. T. & S. F. Ry. — 0.3
.11			10.51	9.16	9.06		4.11	488.6	DODSWORTH — 0.6
								489.2	Crossing P. E. Ry. — 0.9
.14			s10.54	s 9.19 AM	s 9.09		s 4.14 AM	490.1	D-R **FLORENCE** — 1.0
								491.1	ARDMORE — 1.8
								492.9	Crossing S. P., L. A & S. L. Ry. — 0.2
.19			f 11.00		f 9.15			493.1	CUDAHY — 1.1
			f		f			494.2	VINVALE — 1.8
.25			s11.07		s 9.22			496.0	D DOWNEY — 2.4
.30 PM			s11.12		s 9.27			498.4	R **STUDEBAKER** — 1.7
			s11.17		s 9.32			500.1	D NORWALK — 2.1
			f11.21		f 9.36			502.2	CARMENITA — 3.2
			s11.28		s 9.43			505.4	D BUENA PARK — 1.0
			f11.30		9.45			506.4	ALMOND — 1.7
			f11.33		f 9.48			508.1	BROOKSHURST — 1.9
			s11.38		s 9.53			510.0	D-R **WEST ANAHEIM**
	12.10 PM							510.0	D-R **WEST ANAHEIM** — 2.0
	*12.19							512.0	MIRAFLORES — 1.1
	12.25 PM							513.1	R **WEST ANAHEIM JUNC.**
		12.15 PM	11.38		9.53			510.0	D-R **WEST ANAHEIM** — 1.2
		s12.20	s11.42		s 9.57			511.2	D ANAHEIM — 1.7
		12.25 PM	s11.46		s10.01			512.9	R **TUSTIN JUNC.** — 1.0
			11.48		10.03			513.9	**WEST ANAHEIM JUNC.** — 1.7
			f11.52		f10.06			515.6	WEST ORANGE — 1.5
								517.1	Crossing P. E. Ry. — 0.9
			11.59 AM		s10.15	7.30 AM		518.0	D-R **SANTA ANA** — 0.1
								518.1	Crossing S. A. & N. Ry. — 4.3
					f10.25	f 7.42		522.4	PAULARINO (Spur) — 3.1
					f10.30	f 7.49		525.5	THURIN — 1.2
					f10.34	f 7.53		526.7	HARPER — 2.3
								529.0	Crossing P. E. Ry. — 0.2
					10.40 AM	8.05 AM		529.2	D-R **NEWPORT BEACH**
Daily Ex. Sunday — Arrive	Arrive Wednesday Only	Arrive Daily Ex. Sunday and Wed.	Arrive Daily	Arrive Daily	Arrive Daily	Arrive Daily Ex. Sunday	Arrive Daily		(44.5)
(0.30)	(0.15)	(0.10)	(1.19)	(0.14)	(1.45)	(0.35)	(0.14)		............Total Time.........
7.20	12.28	29.00	25.29	23.14	25.42	19.20	23.14		.........Average Speed per Hour.....

(Double Track — Los Angeles to West Anaheim)

72. Exceptions—No. 392 is superior to No. 391. No. 120 is superior to No. 119.

Eastward From San Francisco						TIME TABLE No. 107 September 1, 1910		Toward San Francis	
Length of sidings in feet, and location of Scales, Fuel, Water & Turning Stations.	FIRST CLASS			Distance from San Francisco.			Distance from Alamitos Beach.	SECOND CL	
	174 Long Beach Passenger	170 San Pedro Passenger	396 Long Beach Motor			STATIONS		397 Long Beach Motor	171 Long Beach Passenger
	Leave Daily	Leave Daily	Leave Daily					Arrive Daily	Arrive Daily
4,699 Y	4.10 PM	10.15 AM	5.10 AM	502.4	R	THENARD	3.8	6.40 AM	11.10 AM
				503.3		Crossing P. E. Ry. 0.9	2.9		
300				503.6		BIRD (Spur) 0.3	2.6		
				505.5		Crossing P. E. Ry. 1.9	0.7		
	▪4.20	▪10.25	s 5.25	505.7	D-R	LONG BEACH 0.2	0.5	s 6.30	s11.00
				505.8		Crossing P. E. Ry. 0.1	0.4		
3,897 T	4.25 PM	10.30 AM	5.30 AM	506.2		ALAMITOS BEACH 0.4	0.0	6.10 AM	10.40 AM
				506.4		Crossing S. P., L. A. & S. L. Ry. 0.2			
	Arrive Daily	Arrive Daily	Arrive Daily			(3.8)		Leave Daily	Leave Daily
	(0.15) 15.18	(0.15) 15.18	(0.20) 11.40			..........Total Time.......... ...Average speed per hour...		(0.30) 7.60	(0.30) 7.60

Westward trains are superior to trains of
Exceptions—No. 140 is superior

Westward trains must procure clearance at Long Beach and San Pedro, when operator on duty.

COAST BRANCHES SUBDIVISION (continued)

Eastward From San Francisco					TIME TABLE No. 107 September 1, 1910		Toward S. Fran. W		
Length of sidings in feet, and location of Scales, Fuel, Water and Turning Stations.	FIRST CLASS		282 Mixed	Distance from San Francisco.		Distance from Los Alamitos.	FIRST CLASS		Tel Office
					STATIONS		271 Mixed	287 Mixed	
			Leave Daily Ex. Sunday				Arrive Daily Ex. Sunday	Arrive Daily Ex. Sunday	
3,560 YW			9.55 AM	510.0	D-R WEST ANAHEIM 1.3	9.4	9.30 AM	11.55 AM	7.00 AM
			f10.00	511.3	NEFF (Spur) 1.0	8.1	f 9.25	f11.50	
512			f10.03	512.3	NUTWOOD 2.3	7.1	f 9.22	f11.47	
1,790			f10.08	514.6	BENEDICT 0.4	4.	f 9.17	f11.42	
				515.0	Crossing P. E. Ry. 0.1	4.4			
Y			10.10	515.1	R BENEDICT JUNC. 4.3	4.3	9.15 AM	11.40	
14,370 TWO			10.20 AM	519.4	D-R LOS ALAMITOS	0.0		11.30 AM	7.00 AM
			Arrive Daily Ex. Sunday		(9.4)		Leave Daily Ex. Sunday	Leave Daily Ex. Sunday	
			(0.25) 22.32		..........Total Time.......... ...Average speed per hour...		(0.15) 20.40	(0.25) 22.32	

Westward trains are superior to trains of the same class in the op

Trains must procure clearance at West Anaheim, when operator on duty.

Los Angeles Div.

COAST BRANCHES SUBDIVISION (continued)

est.	Eastward	From S. Fran							Toward S. Fran. West.	
	Length of sidings in feet, and location of Scales, Fuel, Water and Turning Stations.	FIRST CLASS		Distance from San Francisco.	TIME TABLE No. 107 September 1, 1910		Distance from Tustin.	SECOND CLASS		
		278 Mixed						279 Mixed		
		Leave Daily Ex. Sunday			STATIONS			Arrive Daily Ex. Sunday		
		12.25 PM		512.9	R **TUSTIN JUNC**		10.5	2.00 PM		
	I			513.4	0.5 Crossing A. T. & S. F. Ry.		10.0			
	1,258	f12.31		515.5	2.1 MARLBORO		7.9	f 1.54		
	I			515.8	0.3 Crossing A. T. & S. F. Ry.		7.6			
6.00PM	846	f12.37		517.7	1.9 WANDA		5.7	f 1.48		
	1,050	s12.50		519.4	1.7 MCPHERSON		4.0	s 1.40		
	1,140	f12.55		520.4	1.0 EL MODENA		3.0	f 1.30		
	4,628	T 1.05 PM		523.4	3.0 R **TUSTIN**		0.0	1.20 PM		
		Arrive Daily Ex. Sunday			(10.5)			Leave Daily Ex. Sunday		

(0.40)	Total Time....	(0.40)
15.75	Average speed per hour	15.75

...ass in the opposite direction. See Rule 72.
No. 394 is superior to No. 395.

Los Angeles Div.

COAST BRANCHES SUBDIVISION (continued)

...stward	From San Francisco						Toward S. Fran. West.		
	Length of sidings... feet, and location of Scales, Fuel, Water and Turning Stations.	FIRST CLASS		Distance from San Francisco	TIME TABLE No. 107 September 1, 1910	Distance from Newport Beach	FIRST CLASS		Telegraph Office Hours
							271 Mixed		
					STATIONS		Arrive Daily Ex. Sunday		
Y				515.1	R **BENEDICT JUNC.**	15.8	9.15 AM		
				518.4	3.3 WESTMINSTER	12.5	f 9.05		
				519.9	1.5 SUGAR	11.1			
				520.5	0.6 SMELTZER	10.4	s 9.00		
W				521.5	1.0 WINTERSBURG	9.4	s 8.50		
				522.9	1.4 WIEBLING	8.0	f 8.45		
				523.4	0.5 LA BOLSA	7.5	f 8.43		
				523.8	0.4 WESTFALL	7.1	f 8.40		
				524.3	0.5 NEWLAND	6.6	f 8.35		
				525.4	1.1 HUNTINGTON BEACH	5.5	s 8.30		
				525.5	0.1 Crossing P. E. Ry.	5.4			
				527.3	1.8 SAND SPUR	3.6			
				530.7	3.4 Crossing P. E. Ry.	0.2			
WY				530.9	0.2 D-R **NEWPORT BEACH**	0.0	8.15 AM		7.00AM to 7.00PM
					(15.8)		Leave Daily Ex. Sunday		

	Total Time	(1.00)
	Average speed per hour	15.80

...tion. See Rule 72. Exceptions—No. 282 is superior to No. 287.

Oil production contributed greatly to
railroad freight volume in the early 1900s.
The prolific Olinda field caused the Santa Fe
to build a long spur into this foothill
district, whose wells became a major source
of fuel oil for Santa Fe steam locomotives.
This view of the Olinda field, taken about
1910, shows the tank car loading racks at
extreme right.
– First American Title Company

6 Orange County Comes Of Age
Railroads In The Era Of Industry And Urbanization

Orange County's railroads helped lead the change from an agricultural economy into an urban and industrial economy, the County having a growth rate unsurpassed by any other in the nation in the decades following World War Two. Major developments which impacted the railroads of the county included oil production, provision of construction materials, military installations, and, ultimately, the evolution of modern industrial parks. The rapid pace of urbanization of the 1970s also sparked a revival of rail passenger service.

Rail Services for the Oil Industry

For decades, Orange County's best known business was agriculture but there were other industries that were important to the county and its railroads. Indeed, the county's most valuable product for many years was petroleum, and this commodity — like the products of the county's soil — produced some significant railroad activity.

"Brea," otherwise known as tar, was discovered in the hills northeast of Anaheim as early as the 1880s. The heavy, sticky material was hauled by wagon to the Southern Pacific depot in Anaheim for transshipment. At the same time, kerosene and related petroleum distillates were received at Anaheim in tank car lots for distribution by mule-drawn tank wagons to communities in the Santa Ana Valley. The railroads themselves experimented with oil for locomotive fuel during the 1890s, and by 1905 both steam railroads in Orange County had converted most of their motive power to oil fuel.

Flowing crude oil was successfully produced in the Puente Hills in north Orange County in the 1890s. In 1899 the Santa Fe built a four mile long branch from Richfield (Atwood) north to Olinda in the booming Brea-Olinda oil district. A small depot was established beside the oil camp near the end of the line at a site today occupied by Carbon Canyon Regional Park. A quarter of a mile beyond, loading racks were built to enable a dozen tank cars to be filled at one time. This branch never had regular passenger service but for several years scheduled daily freight service carried oilfield equipment, materials and supplies inbound and petroleum outbound. Some of the crude oil exported was consigned to local refineries but much was used, even without refining, as locomotive boiler fuel. In fact the Santa Fe Railway held a proprietary interest in some of the output from the Olinda field through ownership of one of the major production companies, and for some years this field was a major source of fuel oil for the Santa Fe System.

This view of the Richfield (Atwood) district along the Santa Fe Railway shows the forest of derricks marking the great Richfield-East Placentia oil field discovered in 1919. This circa 1924 view shows Santa Fe's Atwood depot, built in 1921, the second station on this site.
— Cochem and Ron Sands (Historical Panormics of Orange County)

Richfield station on the Santa Fe was the birthplace of what was to become one of the nation's major oil companies. In 1911, Thaddeus Winter, F.R. Kellogg, and four partners already engaged in the refining business in Los Angeles organized the Richfield Oil Company. This new company built a small topping plant (an early form of distillation refinery designed to remove only the top, or light fractions of crude oil) adjacent to the wye track at Richfield. The Richfield refinery was intended to "top" crude oil purchased from the Santa Fe Railway and delivered from their wells in the Olinda field. Later the fledgling company also bought tank car lots from independent producers all over north Orange County. Richfield Oil grew from these small beginnings to become one of the largest independent oil companies on the Pacific Coast. In 1965, it joined with an Eastern firm to become the Atlantic Richfield Company (now ARCO). From its earliest days, when it relied upon the Santa Fe to supply it with crude oil for its original refinery, Richfield Oil had a close relationship with Southern California's railroads; throughout the steam era it was a major supplier of locomotive fuel in the region.

As demand for petroleum products increased during the first quarter of the Twentieth Century, oil companies established "bulk plants" to handle wholesale and retail distribution of their refined products. At the plants, 42-

The Huntington Beach oil field boomed in the 1920s, and was largely located along the two miles of SP-PE joint track between La Bolsa and the coast. This view was taken at Westfall Station and shows how Summit Avenue was closed to permit the construction and operation of side tracks to serve loading platforms.
– Huntington Beach Public Library

Thanks to the oil boom and subsequent growth in the City of Huntington Beach, once-bucolic Newland station on the joint PE/SP La Bolsa line became a busy shipping place in the 1920s. This mid-1940s view shows a P.E. electric locomotive with a single boxcar headed south towards the coast.
– Jack Ferrier photo, Richard Fellows Collection

and 55-gallon drums and tank car loads of petroleum products could be unloaded and stored against demand; tall storage tanks were the customary landmark of these facilities. Important bulk plants were established on rail spurs at Fullerton, Brea, Anaheim, Santa Ana, Garden Grove, Huntington Beach, Newport Beach, Tustin, Irvine, and San Juan. The major refined products shipped into the county included lubricants, kerosene, agricultural sprays, heavy fuel oils, and fuels for orchard "smudge pot" heaters. As the county became more mechanized after the First World War, motor oils and fuels and oil-based paving materials joined the list of petroleum products received by rail.

As new oil discoveries were made at La Habra, north of Fullerton, and along the coast, spurs were put in along existing rail lines to accommodate the growing production. Los Coyotes field in northwest Orange County was developed by Standard Oil in the 1910s, using supplies shipped to Des Moines Station on the Pacific Electric and to points along the La Habra Valley Spur built by the Santa Fe. By 1914, oil production from north Orange County fields exceeded a million barrels each month, and was worth over $10 million annually. This value was greater than for any other single county product and represented one third of the value of all county products combined.

The greatest county oil discoveries were yet to come, however. Running beneath the ground from Newport Beach northwest to Seal Beach is a geological structure containing several important oil deposits. Attempts were first made to tap these deposits as early as 1899, when drilling was done on the mesa above Newport. The attempt was not successful and many years were to elapse before commercial quantities of oil were brought into production from this field. Much more dramatic was the discovery of oil in nearby Huntington Beach. In 1920, oil was discovered on the Huntington Beach mesa, inland from the town. The first well was spudded in (drilled) on May 24th within sight of the La Bolsa sugar factory. One year later there were twelve wells in operation, producing 8,000 barrels per day. Three months after that, 42 wells were producing and by October production was generating 200 car loads of oil traffic per month. By April of 1923 there were 150 wells in the Huntington Beach field producing 124,000 barrels daily.

These were boom times in Orange County's newest "oil patch." A virtual forest of oil derricks dotted the landscape as every town lot owner sought his share of the riches. Both the S.P. and the P.E. enjoyed a significant increase in freight business as a result. Sidings and spurs were put in at almost every available space along the joint track between the ocean front and La Bolsa station, and P.E. even built a spur line up one of the side streets at the west end of town. All of this spur construction was to accommodate the volume of incoming drilling pipe, machinery, and construction materials, and to ship out the ocean of "black gold" which flowed from the loading racks constructed alongside the tracks. (One of these loading racks was the largest in the county at that time and could handle 30 cars simultaneously.) The Pacific Electric benefitted not only from shipping oil but also from owning land which produced oil.

In response to this booming business along the branch, in 1921 the S.P. erected a permanent freight station at La Bolsa to replace the old boxcar which had housed the agency since 1918. At one time this busy agency accounted for more than 200 car loads of traffic *each day*, comprised of beets, other vegetables, sugar, and oil-related traffic. Southern Pacific's old Smeltzer Branch, characterized twenty years earlier as a weed-grown cow pasture, had become a busy, multi-tracked industrial line traversed both by steam trains and — as far as La Bolsa — by electric freight trains and trolley cars. Passage of the trains of the two companies over this congested trackage was regulated by an electric staff system.

This surge in traffic was not without incident. In one case a fire was started on an oil spur by a spark from one of P.E.'s electric locomotives. On another occasion a hasty effort to unload a car of oil well pipe in the path of an approaching freight train resulted in tragedy. A "gin pole" had been rigged to

One of Orange County's worst railway calamities occurred near Yorba Station on the Santa Fe Railway on August 4, 1915. A runaway tank car loaded with oil roared down the Olinda Spur and eastbound onto the main line into Santa Ana Canyon. At an estimated closing speed of 100 mph, the tanker crashed into a westbound local passenger train en route from San Bernardino, killing three crewmen and injuring many passengers.
– Anaheim Public Library

unload the pipe at La Bolsa and a supporting guy wire had accidentally been stretched across the track. As the morning Southern Pacific freight train approached, the La Bolsa agent realized the danger and ran out to stop the train but it was too close. The smokestack of the steam locomotive snagged the guy wire, pulling down the pole and spilling the load of pipe, killing one workman.

The busy oil traffic on Santa Fe's Olinda spur was the cause of perhaps the most dramatic railroad accident ever to take place within Orange County. On August 4, 1915, a loaded oil tank car got away from the Santa Fe switch crew working the loading racks at Olinda. The car quickly picked up speed on the steeply-graded branch line, catching the staff at Richfield (Atwood) entirely by surprise as it rolled off the branch, around the east leg of the wye, and entered the main line heading east towards Santa Ana Canyon. Unfortunately, a westbound passenger train had already passed the last open agency station before Richfield and so could not be kept out of harm's way. Tragedy struck when the wayward oil car, travelling eastbound at an estimated 60 miles per hour and the unsuspecting train, moving west at 40 miles per hour, collided head-on with a terrific impact near Yorba station. The tank car ruptured, spraying the flammable contents onto the hot steam locomotive and resulting in a holocaust which engulfed and destroyed the entire train. Three crewmen were killed, thirty passengers were seriously injured, and all that was left of the train after the fire was a scorched locomotive, twisted metal framing and the ashes of the wooden coaches. This spectacular accident received attention from the national media including even *Scientific American.*

Despite these tragic and sometimes spectacular accidents, railroad involvement in Orange County's petroleum industry was generally beneficial. The production and transportation of this commodity boosted train operations, increased the value of rail exports from the county, and generally stimulated the economy. Oil traffic peaked on the county's rails in the latter 1920s, however, as pipelines were laid to transport petroleum products in greater volume than tank cars could handle. Early pipelines were owned by the oil companies but eventually two of the county's railroads formed a company to build and operate the major petroleum products pipeline running through the county. Jointly owned by the Southern Pacific and the Santa Fe, the San Diego Pipeline Company's pipe uses the right of way of Espee's Santa Ana line and (former) Tustin branch, and Santa Fe's San Diego line, through the county. It carries thousands of barrels of aircraft and motor vehicle fuels daily from southern Los Angeles County to markets in Orange and San Diego Counties.

Sand and Gravel Traffic

Over the years sand, gravel, rock, and clay have also contributed substantial tonnages to the county's railroads. Earlier (see chapter 5) it was mentioned that the Espee installed a spur between Newport and Huntington Beach where sand was loaded for use in Los Angeles Division locomotives. For years, El Toro station on the Santa Fe originated many carloads of clay which came from a deposit in the nearby foothills. South and east of Orange the Espee, the Pacific Electric, and the Santa Fe all had spurs along Santiago Creek from which gravel was shipped at various times. Some of this rock was used as ballast along the railroad companies' lines but much was loaded for commercial sale elsewhere.

At least two of these commercial sand and gravel operations in Orange County were large enough to support their own industrial railroads. It is not known if any of these companies ever had steam locomotives but all were early users of gasoline-mechanical locomotives. The Orange County Rock and Gravel Company had 36-inch narrow gauge trackage at their "McPherson Plant" which processed materials removed from the bed of Santiago Creek. Most of this plant's output was shipped out via S.P.'s Tustin Branch. In 1927, this company was purchased by Union Rock and two years later became a part of Consolidated Rock (Conrock) Company. Conrock continued extraction operations at this facility until about 1970. Rail shipments of rock products over S.P.'s Tustin Branch ended when the line was cut back to Villa Park in 1969 as a result of the washout of the bridge over Santiago Creek.

Table 6.1
Locomotive Roster
Orange County Rock and Gravel Company
McPherson Plant, Orange, California

(All locomotives 36-inch gauge; no road numbers known)

OCR&G Purchase	Builder	Number	Model	Weight (Tons)	Notes
1922	Plymouth	1186	BL	7	(1)
1922	Plymouth	1324	BL	7	(2)
1923	Plymouth	1414	DL	7	(3)
1923	Plymouth	1532	DL	7	(4)
1923	Plymouth	1560	DL	7	(5)
1924	Plymouth	1670	DL	7	(6)

Notes:

(1)   Purchased new (03-1922); sold to Clark Rock & Gravel Co., L.A. (02-15-1924).

(2)   Purchased new from dealer (12-30-22); sold to Fenton-Parker Materials, San Diego (02-13-25).

(3)   Purchased new (03-1923); still in service 1931; disposition unknown.

(4)   Previously owned by Santiago Creek Rock & Gravel Co. (new 08-1923); acquired from equipment dealer H.C. Collins (12-20-23); disposition unknown.

(5)   Purchased new (08-1923); still in service, 1931; disposition unknown.

(6)   Purchased new from dealer (05-28-24); still in service, 1931; disposition unknown.

(Source: Joseph A. Strapac)

The Yaeger Rock Company operated 30-inch narrow gauge tracks at their facility in the City of Orange. In January 1927, the Yaeger plant was purchased by Union Rock and the facility apparently closed prior to 1931. A third company, Santiago Creek Rock and Gravel Company of Anaheim, may also have operated 36-inch gauge tracks at a plant in the early 1920s, but nothing is known of the history of this facility.

Table 6.2
Locomotive Roster
Yaeger Rock Company
Orange, California

(All locomotives 30-inch gauge; no road numbers known)

Yaeger Purchase	Builder	Number	Model	Weight (Tons)	Notes
1922	Whitcomb	11383	UF	3.5	(1)
1925	Whitcomb	12055	UF	4.0	(2)

Notes:

(1) Purchased new (06-1922); disposition unknown.

(2) Purchased new (09-1925); disposition unknown.

(Source: Joseph A. Strapac)

Although Orange County was blessed with commercial deposits of sand, gravel, and clay, when large-sized durable stone was needed for special construction projects it had to be imported from outside Orange County, and the railroads were generally the most efficient land-based carriers for this type of traffic. The railroads were often their own customers, importing car loads of large "rip-rap" rocks to protect rights of way threatened with erosion.

In addition to these "rock trams" there was another industrial-type railroad in Orange County. The Western Salt Company operated a 24-inch gauge line to haul salt from several evaporating ponds at the head of Upper Newport Bay to a processing and cleaning facility located near the present intersection of Backbay Drive and East Bluff Drive in Newport Beach. This operation, which used one Plymouth gasoline locomotive and a dozen or so side-dump cars, ran along the tops of the dikes separating the various salt ponds. It existed from 1934 until 1969 when the salt works was washed out in a heavy storm. The locomotive and cars were then transferred to another salt works in San Diego owned by the same company.

Building the County's Infrastructure

The development of Newport Harbor either for shipping or pleasure craft was an important priority for the people of Newport Beach and for the County of Orange. After assistance at the Federal level was repeatedly thwarted, harbor improvement became one of the major public improvement projects undertaken by the county's own citizens in the decade following World War I. A significant tonnage of quarried stone was carried by rail to Newport Harbor in conjunction with the construction of the jetties at the harbor entrance.

Some work was done on the west jetty in 1917 and again in 1921, but a major attempt to improve the harbor came in 1927 after the city of Newport Beach voted to spend $500,000 on the project. Rocks for the jetty came from quarries at Declezville, near Riverside, and were transported to the Newport jetty by the Southern Pacific and Pacific Electric. The S.P. carried the rock into Orange County and down to Newport via the former SA&N tracks. In Newport Beach a track connection was reestablished between the S.P. and the P.E., the earlier connection having been removed in 1923 when the Southern Pacific finally abandoned the Newport Wharf and associated trackage. Pacific Electric extended its Balboa track from the terminus at Main Street out to the end of the peninsula. This trackage was not electrified, and a P.E. steam switcher was used to shove the cars of rock out to the jetty. Loaded flat cars started arriving at the beach in June of 1927 and continued to be delivered at an average of 30 cars a day for the remainder of the year. By the end of the year, slightly more than 3,000 carloads — aggregating 150,000 tons — had been hauled through the county and dumped into the ocean to improve the west jetty.

The jetty work and other improvements at Newport stirred local hopes for renewed maritime commerce there. These feelings were elevated by visits from officials of the Espee, the Santa Fe, and the U.P. In 1927, Southern Pacific built a new depot at Newport, sharing it jointly with the P.E. At this time, an Espee spokesmen declared that the railroad was "for Newport Harbor, first, last, and all time," a statement that must have made James McFadden turn over in his grave!

In fact, the freight business which came to the new county dock on the bay went entirely to trucks, so a planned spur track to it was never built. Espee's business at Newport continued to decline, from 45,000 tons during the first half of 1923 (primarily inbound construction materials) to only 8,000 tons in 1928 and to less than a thousand tons in 1932. Faced with this loss of business (and with the reality that Newport was going to develop into a harbor for pleasure craft), the Southern Pacific took steps to abandon the former Santa Ana & Newport track from Dyer (south of Santa Ana) to Newport and Huntington Beach. What had once been the county's only prosperous independent short line became a casualty of the nation-wide depression when, in 1933, the I.C.C. granted its approval to abandon the trackage. As a condition of the abandonment, S.P. retained the right to operate freight trains over the parallel Pacific Electric line between Newport and Huntington Beach if necessary.

Development of other parts of the county's infra-structure also contributed traffic to the local railroads. Construction materials in general, including lumber, cement, pipe for water and sewer systems, telephone and power poles, and paving materials all contributed to periodic surges in rail traffic. In 1924, for example, large quantities of concrete aggregate were delivered by the S.P. to a temporary spur along the beach to facilitate the construction of the Pacific Coast Highway between Huntington Beach and Newport. To distribute this material up and down the length of the five-mile long paving project over soft sand, the contractor set up a temporary narrow gauge railroad parallel to, but inland of, the Southern Pacific track. This temporary contractor's railroad was the fourth rail line to have been put down along this stretch of beach and sand dune. At this point, the original Santa Ana & Newport Railway had been laid closer to the ocean than either of the then-existing tracks of the S.P. or the P.E.

Storm Damage

The northern and western sections of Orange County are subject to repeated flooding from the Santa Ana River and other streams which traverse the coastal plain. It will be recalled that heavy rains damaged the Southern Pacific's tracks within days of the opening of the line to Anaheim in 1875 (see Chapter 1). It has also been mentioned (see Chapter 4) that Pacific Electric's Santa Ana-Huntington Beach line was permanently severed following the washout of its Santa Ana River crossing in 1922. Periodic flooding and washouts plagued the county's railroads; the worst damage in the Nineteenth Century was done in 1884, 1889, and 1891; the worst storms of the Twentieth Century came in 1916, 1938 and 1969.

The storms of 1916 drenched the whole of Southern California from mid-January into February. The Santa Ana River could not be contained within its banks, and washed out railroad trestles and bridges at six points in Orange County. Four more bridges were damaged or destroyed by Santiago Creek. Flooding in normally dry Coyote Creek in the north county and San Juan Creek in the south also damaged rail crossings. Rail communications to the county's major communities, Santa Ana, Orange, Anaheim, Tustin, Fullerton, Newport and San Juan were effectively cut off.

By the time the sky had cleared, nearly every railroad bridge in the county had been washed out or damaged enough to prevent safe use. The worst damage was done to the trackage of the S.P. and the P.E. along the ocean front between Huntington Beach and Newport when the rain-swollen Santa Ana River (which in those days flowed into the western arm of Newport Bay) broke through the barrier of coastal sand dunes. This breakthrough carried away over 1,000 feet of trackage of both railroads about one mile southeast of Huntington Beach.

Fortunately, Southern Pacific's trestle at the foot of the Newport Mesa withstood the storm, and the ex-SA&N line to Santa Ana remained open. Boats carrying milk and meat landed at the ocean wharf at Newport, and critical supplies were carried by rail up to Santa Ana until inland rail connections were restored.

The repair job itself was massive, slowed by mainline railroad damage over a wide area of Southern California. Southern Pacific's line to Santa Ana was reopened briefly but quickly washed out again. It was finally reopened for a second time only after pile drivers could be released from repair work on the company's transcontinental lines. The Pacific Electric and the Santa Fe each required a full week to restore service between Los Angeles and Santa Ana, but Santa Fe service to San Diego was not restored until three weeks later. P.E.'s Santa Ana-Huntington Beach line was also severed and did not reopen until May.

It was April before Pacific Electric resumed partial service on its line to Newport. Repair work began to repair the 1,000-foot long washout southeast of Huntington Beach in February when a work train was dispatched via S.P.'s Westminster line. Working from the west side of the gap, a pile driver began construction of a 1,200-foot trestle, punching over 300 35-foot piles twenty feet into the underlying clay strata. With four piles per bent, and each bent fifteen feet apart, the work went slowly yet it was of a "decidedly permanent nature" so the finished bridge could be used by both electric trains and steam trains, if desired.

Pacific Electric's rails were reconnected and partial service resumed in April of 1916, but the Southern Pacific waited for more than two years to reconnect its track. This disrupted the operations of both companies over that important coastal stretch for a protracted period. Even after the Southern Pacific did restore its steam train service, it did not lay its own track but simply connected with the P.E. track on either side and used the rails of the trolley company across the trestle. Hand thrown signals were installed to coordinate the use of the single track trestle, and because the switches were normally set for the Southern Pacific, there was a six minute delay to each of the 30 Pacific Electric trains which daily travelled the Newport line at that time.

Prior to the construction of Prado Dam, heavy rainfalls frequently resulted in flooding in Orange County. The worst flooding came in 1938. This aerial view shows the Southern Pacific depot grounds and beet loading ramp at Buena Park under several feet of water, along with the businesses on Beach Boulevard in the foreground.
– First American Title Company

During the next two years, county officials decided to permanently divert the Santa Ana River into the ocean between Huntington Beach and Newport but a channel route was selected which ran east of the Pacific Electric trestle just described. When the new channel was first cut, a large culvert was placed under the tracks of each railroad company. The Pacific Electric then built another trestle at this location but the Southern Pacific continued to rely on its culvert. Then in March of 1921 a storm washed out S.P.'s culvert. Rather than repair this second washout the steam road bypassed the break by again tying into the P.E. track. Because the S.P. had never restored its own track over the site of the original 1916 washout, this now made two locations along the coast where S.P.'s steam trains were shunted onto the electric tracks with corresponding slowing of trolley service. It was not until 1925 that the two railroad companies agreed to remove the hand-operated protective signals on each side of the two trestles and to permit P.E.'s trolleys to run through without stopping, leaving it up to the by now rather infrequent steam trains to flag their occasional way across the joint bridges.

The flood of 1938, the worst in the county's history, caused a repeat of the washouts, bridge failures, and rail line closures experienced as a result of the 1916 storm. Weeks were again required to restore the county's rail network to normal. One of the major outcomes of that year's flood devastation was the immediate commencement of construction of Prado Dam at the upper end of Santa Ana Canyon just outside Orange County. This large project included a major relocation of the Santa Fe Railway immediately east of the point where it crossed into Orange County. As a result of this line change three sidetrack stations — Chester, Greda and Prado (the latter originally named Rincon, then Crary, later Cota, and still later Quivero) — were abandoned and one new sidetrack station (Prado Dam) was established.

Impact of Two World Wars and Lesser Conflicts

Both the First and Second World Wars produced significant changes to Orange County's rail operations. World War I, fought primarily in Europe, caused a disproportionate share of the nation's railroad cars to be concentrated in the East. The subsequent congestion in East Coast ports resulted in western railroads and western shippers being deprived of an adequate supply of railroad cars. Because of this shortage, and to facilitate the workings of the national railroad system in support of the defense effort, steam railroads (but not electric lines) were nationalized by President Wilson on December 20, 1917.

Federal management was carried out by the United States Railroad Administration and the dictates of this agency quickly impacted every aspect of railroad operation. In Orange County the U.S.R.A. "rationalized" local steam railroad passenger services by eliminating some local services and consolidating others at places where more than one railroad had been providing service. Federal mandates also pushed more efficient utilization of railroad equipment and facilities, and some of these changes, such as heavier car loading and reductions in local passenger schedules, continued even after the railroads were returned to their owners in 1920. The volume of traffic carried over Orange County's rail lines during World War I was heavier than normal and the largest

In the late 1950s, Pacific Electric crews operated the Huntington Beach local with SP equipment and carried loads to be handed over to the U.S. Navy Railroad, destined for the Seal Beach Navy base. In this view of the junction between the two railroads in Westminster, unofficially known as "Ammo Junction," USN No. 2 is awaiting cars from the local freight at left.
– Willis Hendrick

In January 1961, a maintenance crew at the Seal Beach Naval Weapons Center repaints one of the "Navy Railroad's" diesels at the engine house on the base.
– U.S. Navy

known movement was the passage of the 40th Division, U.S. Army, from Camp Kearney in San Diego to the East Coast in the Summer of 1918. This movement over the Santa Fe consisted of 56 trains and apparently took several days to complete. Each train averaged 8 hours and 30 minutes to make the journey from San Diego to Barstow.

The Second World War had an even more profound effect upon western railroads and a direct impact on the Orange County landscape. Rail spurs were put in to such new military installations as the Marine Corps Air Station at El Toro and the Navy's Lighter Than Air Station south of Tustin (now the Marine Helicopter Station-Tustin), both of which were served by the Santa Fe Railway. The Santa Ana Army Air Base, located on what is now the Orange County Fairgrounds and the campus of Orange Coast College in Costa Mesa, was served (for freight traffic only) by a spur built southward from disused Pacific Electric trackage west of Greenville on the old Santa Ana-Huntington Beach line. P.E. also served the Naval Ammunition and Net Depot at Seal Beach, this facility causing a substantial disruption of services on the company's Newport line (see Chapter 4).

Troop trains and military materiel moved in unprecedented volume to the county's defense facilities, and through the county to the Pacific Fleet Navy Base and other military camps in San Diego. These trains carried everything from troops and ammunition to helium for balloons and blimps. Late in the war as many as 49 trains *a day* were recorded passing through Orange Station on the Santa Fe Railway. To accomodate this heavy flow of traffic the Santa Fe made significant improvements to its signalling and track in the county. Double track was opened between La Mirada and Fullerton on May 10, 1943. Centralized Traffic Control (CTC) was activated between Fullerton and Venta on October 22, 1943, and from Venta to San Diego on July 4, 1944. CTC was activated between between Fullerton and Esperanza on April 8, 1945, and on the Olive District on September 10, 1945. The control boards for the Orange County sections of the CTC installations were originally placed in the second story of the Fullerton Depot; later they were moved to San Bernardino.

Each of the military bases in the county was furnished with its own diesel-electric locomotives for on-base switching purposes, but the huge Seal Beach ammunition facility, which covered 3,000 acres (later 4,000) fronting on Anaheim Bay, was equipped with a complete railroad; there were some 65 miles of track, a fleet of from three to five locomotives at any one time, and more than 100 freight cars. The maze of trackage on the base included 274 turnouts (switches) and separate spurs to service each of the more than 100 bunkers, magazines and storage tracks on the base.

Table 6.3
Locomotive Roster
Naval Ammunition & Net Depot, Seal Beach
Naval Weapons Station, Seal Beach

| Numbers | | | | Weight | | |
Local	USN Serial	Builder	Number	(Tons)	HP	Notes
1	65-00319	GE	27616	25	150	(1)
2	65-00320	GE	27811	25	150	(2)
3	65-00317	GE	13068	50	300	(3)
4	65-00318	GE	17999	65	400	(4)
(no No. 5 known)						(5)
6	65-00321	Whitcomb	60638	80	unknown	(6)
7	65-00291	Whitcomb	60639	80	unknown	(7)
8	65-00316	Whitcomb	60649	45	unknown	(8)
9	65-00069	Whitcomb	60650	45	unknown	(9)
10	65-00153	Whitcomb	60651	45	unknown	(10)
--	65-00347	GE	31824	80	500	(11)
--	65-00355	GE	31829	80	500	(12)
--	65-00358	GE	31832	80	500	(13)
--	65-00359	GE	31833	80	500	(14)
--	65-00360	GE	31834	80	500	(15)
--	65-00531	Baldwin	67727	120	1200	(16)

Notes:

(1)   Purchased new (08-1944); sold to Holly Sugar Company, Hamilton, California (date unknown).

(2)   Purchased new (08-1944); sold to Diamond National Corporation No. 796 (01-1962).

(3)   Purchased new (03-1941); sold to Soule Steel Company (1964).

(4)   Purchased new (08-1943); in service 1988.

(5)   No locomotive known to have been assigned a local (road) number five.

(6)   Purchased new (06-1945); transferred to Naval Ordinance Test Station, China Lake (date unknown); sold (1969).

(7)   Purchased new (06-1945); sold to Hyman-Michaels No. 7 (1954); sold to Arcata & Mad River No. 103 (1955); sold to Franko Railroad Contractors (06-1960); scrapped at Spokane, Washington (date unknown).

(8)   Purchased new (09-1945); sold to Koppel Bulk Terminals, Long Beach (1965).

(9)   Purchased new (09-1945); in service 1988.

(10)   Purchased new (09-1945); sold to Port of Tillamook Bay No. 2 (1965).

(11)   Built 03-1952; transferred from Port Hueneme (date unknown); in service 1988.

(12)   Built 03-1952; transferred from Naval Air Depot Fallbrook (date unknown); in service 1988.

(13)   Built 04-1953; transferred from Naval Weapons Station, Hawthorne, Nevada (date unknown); in service 1988.

(14)   Built 04-1953; transferred from Naval Weapons Station, Hawthorne, Nevada (date unknown); rebuilt by Chrome Locomotive Company (02 to 11-1986); in service 1988.

(15)   Built 04-1953; transferred from Naval Weapons Station, Hawthorne, Nevada (date unknown); in service 1988.

(16)   Built 07-1943; originally U.S. Army No. 7140, Kendia, New York; transferred to Naval Ammunition Depot, Crane, Indiana (03-1969); rebuilt with EMD engine by Johnson Railway Service, Cornelia, Georgia (10-1980); to NWS, Seal Beach (03-1981); to Naval Weapons Station, Concord (date unknown).

(Source: Joseph A. Strapac)

The Navy's railroad at Seal Beach had two connections to the Orange County rail system. A three-mile long spur was built due east to a junction with Southern Pacific's Smeltzer Branch at Westminster. There was also a connection with the Pacific Electric's Newport line. As was mentioned in Chapter 4, dredging of a channel and construction of wharfage for the new Naval base caused closure of P.E.'s Newport line in 1942. P.E.'s trestle across Anaheim Bay had to be removed and the track relocated to an elevated grade along the inland shore to accommodate the Navy wharf and its lead tracks. This created one of the few instances in Orange County of a fully separated grade crossing between two railroads.

Activity at the Seal Beach facility increased as the Pacific campaigns progressed. Towards the end of 1944 the base railroad had four locomotives to shuffle ordnance and other war materiel and two more were added in June of 1945 in preparation for the invasion of Japan. Due to the atomic bombing of Japanese cities this invasion became unnecessary. At the end of the war activities at Seal Beach subsided, ending in 1946. The base was reactivated for the Korean conflict in 1950, however, and has remained active ever since. In 1962 a deep water channel was dredged to permit aircraft carrier-sized vessels to come up to the wharf for loading, thus reducing the cost of lightering ammunition out to larger vessels.

During the Southeast Asian conflict of the 1960s and 1970s, two or three ships were serviced at Seal Beach every day — more than 600 ships each year. Three Navy railroad crews worked around the clock, handling from 80 to 100 carloads daily and running up as many as 50 miles each day over the trackage within the base. Over the years there have been some interesting rail moves on or through the Seal Beach Navy Base, including 16-inch shells for the huge guns of *New Jersey* class battleships, and car loads of medium tanks to be placed on ships at the wharf. Special deliveries have also been made to the huge NASA/North American Saturn (rocket) Booster construction facility at the northwest corner of the base, and massive electric generators to the City of Los Angeles Department of Water and Power's steam-electric generating station a mile west of the base in Seal Beach. On Armed Forces Day during the nation's

Bicentennial in 1976, the base railroad transported hundreds of visitors, using converted hospital cars and Strategic Air Command cars, all of which have now been removed.

Following the 1973 explosion of a munitions train at Roseville in northern California, new operating procedures were established for deliveries to the Seal Beach Naval Station. Navy rail crews no longer run out over the long spur to the Southern Pacific interchange at Westminster; rather, the few cars of "commercial" traffic that still come to the base each month are delivered through the base gate by S.P. crews under the close supervision of armed Marine guards. Despite this change there is still a substantial amount of activity on the Navy's railroad on the base in the decade of the 1980s. Two three-man Navy train crews and one four-man maintenance crew work during the weekday, supporting the routine peacetime reconditioning of fleet ammunition. In doing so, the little yellow-painted Navy locomotives move from 15 to 20 of the silver, 40-foot munitions boxcars, running some ten to twenty five miles in the process. In the event of a logistical emergency there are still forty barricaded sidings in the southeast quadrant of the base capable of holding 160 loaded cars, or about 8,000 tons of ordnance.

Table 6.4
Locomotive Roster
Marine Corps Air Station, El Toro

Numbers USN Serial	Builder	Number	Weight (Tons)	HP	Notes
65-00409	GE	17802	45	300	(1)
65-00419	GE	17817	45	300	(2)
USMC Serial					
262098	GE	15060	45	300	(3)

Another locomotive has been assigned to El Toro, but details are lacking.

Notes:

(1)   Built 01-1943; first assigned to Naval Ammunition Depot, Port Chicago, California; transferred to USMCAS El Toro (date unknown); sold to George A. Hill Engineering Corporation (date unknown); sold to La Junta Industrial Park, Colorado (01-1971).

(2)   Purchased new (03-1943); sold to Northern Railway of Costa Rica No. 6, and rebuilt to 42-inch gauge (09-1971).

(3)   Built 11-1941; originally U.S. Army No. 7199; transferred to U.S. Navy No. 65-00534 (date unknown); sold to Pacific Railroad Society (03-02-1988); presently stored in City of Commerce.

(Source: Joseph A. Strapac)

One other military base in Orange County still has some rail operations. The Marine Corps Air Station at El Toro was built in 1943 on land purchased from the Irvine Ranch. During the war the Santa Fe Railway delivered tank cars of aviation fuel as well as carloads of parts and other supplies needed to keep the aircraft flying. While the scale of rail operations at El Toro has never been as great as at Seal Beach, there has been enough activity to justify permanent assignment of a switch locomotive to the base.

The presence of the railroad in close proximity to the El Toro Air Base once resulted in an unexpected physical encounter between an aircraft and a train. On November 20, 1958, an F4D "Skyray" trainer crashed while practicing an emergency landing procedure and slid across the adjoining field onto the Santa Fe main line directly in front of an oncoming southbound "San Diegan" which was travelling at a reported speed of 75 mph. The train braked but collided with the aircraft, derailing the three-unit locomotive and five of its seven cars. The impact cartwheeled the plane which burst into flames and came to rest against the train's lounge car carrying 30 passengers. Miraculously, there

During World War Two, Santa Fe received a large allocation of EMD "FT" freight diesels because of the long stretches of arid country traversed by the railroad. For a short time in the early 1950s, Santa Fe experimented with a lower maintenance, all-blue paint job on these freight work horses. FT No.s 170A and B wear this color scheme as they bring a train into Orange County past the cliffs at the west end of Gypsum Siding in the upper reaches of Santa Ana Canyon, on December 16, 1951.

– Stan Kistler

In a picture that typifies Southern Pacific's Orange County operations in the 1970s and early 1980s, a once-ubiquitous SP SW-1500 hustles a sizeable Costa Mesa local across the Broadway offramp from the Santa Ana Freeway on September 18, 1983.
– Bruce Kelly

were no serious injuries among the 130 passengers and five crewmen on board the train, and the pilot of the jet also survived.

Industrial Activity

Following the Second World War, Southern California entered an age of rapidly accelerating immigration from other parts of the country. While this influx is best seen in terms of population growth, there was also a tremendous relocation of industry. Relatively undeveloped Orange County was a prime relocation target, and the county's railroads were instrumental in promoting industrial development and the resulting freight business. During the 1950s both the Southern Pacific and the Santa Fe, through their real estate and industrial development departments or affiliates, began to acquire large parcels of land next to, or near, existing rail lines for conversion to industrial "parks." The Santa Fe initially focussed on land in industrial districts east and west of Fullerton but later benefitted from extensive development of the major industrial complex on Irvine Ranch land south of Tustin.

The Southern Pacific began its land development program in the county by acquiring a hundred acres in Santa Ana in 1954. Subsequently, the railroad purchased and developed 275 acres in Anaheim in 1956, 125 acres in Orange in 1957, 100 acres in Fullerton beginning in 1957, 475 acres in Buena Park

216

Southern Pacific's "Anaheim Hauler" has been a familiar sight on Santa Ana Boulevard in Anaheim throughout the diesel era. SD-39 road power dominates this 1983 view of the "Hauler" muscling a large portion of this day's quota of freight for Orange County's burgeoning industries.
– Bruce Kelly

and La Palma beginning in 1959, plus 290 acres in adjacent La Mirada and Cerritos. By the latter 1970s the S.P. had assisted over 200 firms to locate along its rail lines in Orange County. The improvements made by these industrial "settlers" amounted to over $350 million and created many new jobs as the county urbanized.

As a result of this increase in industrial activity, especially warehousing and distribution operations, the annual carload business on S.P.'s Orange County lines grew from 16,000 cars in 1958 to nearly 60,000 in 1978. To bypass the congested terminal district in Los Angeles and to speed the movement of rail shipments into Orange County, the Southern Pacific constructed the Puente Cutoff in 1954 to reach its Santa Ana Branch at Studebaker. This "new" line consisted of trackage rights over the Union Pacific from Walnut (now City of Industry) to Whittier Junction, new construction along the east bank of the San Gabriel River to a junction with the former Pacific Electric Yorba Linda line at Los Nietos, and thence south on new tracks built on the right of way of S.P.'s Whittier Branch (previously abandoned in 1942) to a junction with the Santa Ana Branch at Studebaker. Although built entirely outside the county, this new route offered substantial time savings to Southern Pacific trains destined for Orange County.

Three daily "hauler" trains carried Orange County-destined freight cars from Espee's yard in the City of Industry, via the Puente Cut-off, leaving cuts of

In the Twentieth Century, all three Orange County railroads hired workers primarily of Hispanic heritage to perform maintenance and track work. In this view from the mid-1940s, a Santa Fe foreman by the name of Dyer (seated at right) poses with his section crew in Santa Ana. It was workers like these who labored so diligently to alleviate the flood damage of 1938.
– Courtesy Jasper Dyer

Santa Fe "high-wide special" No. 2715 has just exited Orange County at the upper end of Santa Ana Canyon, on the second day of its five-day journey from Los Angeles Harbor to Daggett. This special movement of a 200-ton pressure vessel, destined for Southern California Edison's coal gasification plant near Daggett, was the largest object ever to move by rail in U.S. history.
– William A. Myers

At one time it was common to find several generations of the same family working on the railroad. Santa Fe section foreman Jasper Dyer, seated fourth from left, the son of the man pictured a decade earlier in Santa Ana, poses with his crew on a speeder at Horseshoe Bend in Santa Ana Canyon in the early 1950s.
— Courtesy Jasper Dyer

Santa Fe No. 3364 creeps down the steeply inclined track leading into the San Onofre Nuclear Generating Station with a 100-ton transformer. Even though this location is outside Orange County, many trainloads of construction materials and special components traversed the County's rail lines during the construction of Units 2 and 3 at San Onofre in the 1970s and early 1980s.
— William A. Myers

One warm Fall day in 1983, a trio of General Electric-built U36Cs powers Santa Fe's daily SDX (San Diego-bound freight) over the crest at Milepost 189 near Alicia Parkway in Mission Viejo. This is the highest point of elevation along the entire San Diego line.
– Bruce Kelly

cars at every available siding along the Santa Ana Branch. Inbound food products, paper products, lumber, and chemicals made up nearly 85 percent of this traffic. As many as thirteen switching crews, based primarily in Anaheim, would be assigned to deliver these loads to individual industries throughout the county, while at the same time pulling out empties for removal via returning haulers. The top S.P. customers in Orange County at this time were the *Los Angeles Times* and Freedom Newspapers, General Foods, Humko Products, Hunt-Wesson Foods, Safeway Stores, Lucky Stores, Kelly Springfield Tire Company, Georgia Pacific, Western Kraft Paper Group, J.C. Penney, and Kraft Foods.

During the decade of the 1960s railroad freight terminating or originating in Orange County grew fourfold for all three railroad companies, from an average of 100 cars per day in 1960, to more than 400 cars per day in 1970. The railroads owned 2,300 acres of industrial land and, by adding a maze of spurs and sidings, had accumulated some 450 miles of trackage in the county. The Santa Fe had 85 employees assigned to jobs in Orange County, the S.P. had 50 (including, after 1965, former P.E. employees), and the Union Pacific, 15. Closely matching the Southern Pacific, the Santa Fe Railway bulletined an even dozen crews to do local work in the county, with another crew going on duty every two hours around the clock. These crews were based at the company's local operations headquarters in Fullerton. In addition, increasing volumes of main line freight passed directly through the county *en route* to Los Angeles, San Diego, San Bernardino, and points east.

Abandonments and Reconfiguration

Although the volume of freight traffic declined somewhat following the national recession at the end of the 1970s, local and through freight traffic remained high on most Orange County lines in the decade of the 1980s. This relative prosperity has meant that the mileage of rail line abandonments in the county has been lower than that experienced elsewhere in the nation.

Despite this, there have been some significant line closures and consolidations in the years since World War II. On the Pacific Electric particularly, major abandonments of trackage have occurred in the wake of changing economic conditions within the county. In several instances, what remained of the P.E. system was linked to surviving segments of other lines in ways which gave rise to entirely new patterns of operation. One such reconfiguration resulted in 1948 when P.E. purchased from parent Southern Pacific the by then little-used lines from Stanton to Los Alamitos and Stanton to Huntington Beach. Installation of a connection at the point where P.E.'s Santa Ana line crossed S.P.'s Los Alamitos Branch gave Pacific Electric diesel-powered freight trains an alternate means to reach Huntington Beach and coastal points.

For over a decade after this consolidation of trackage, a single daily Pacific Electric local freight train, usually powered by a Baldwin-built diesel switcher, would travel over these lines in Orange County. Originating at Butte Street Yard in Los Angeles, the train would travel south to Watts and then go down the Santa Ana line to Bellflower, Cypress and Stanton. From this point the train would service industries at West Santa Ana (the terminus of freight service on the Santa Ana line after street running was discontinued in 1955) and Los Alamitos as required. The train would then proceed down to switch the lima bean warehouse at Smeltzer, team tracks and a lumber yard at Huntington, boat distributors at Newport Beach, and Dow Chemical at Seal

Under a gentle rain, Santa Fe CF7 No. 2569 prepares to back out of the Coors Spur in the Irvine Industrial Complex in Tustin. Note the streak of light made by the brakeman's lantern as he walks back inspecting the air brake lines.
– Bruce Kelly

Beach. Counting the return to Los Angeles, the crews who worked this leisurely, meandering run put in long hours on a regular basis. The P.E. maintained agency freight stations at Garden Grove until 1962 and at Lake Street in Huntington Beach until 1970. Both were housed in former passenger stations; the latter was the former ocean-front depot next to the Huntington Beach pier which had been moved to Third and Lake Streets in 1941.

The restoration of regular freight service over the Stanton-Huntington Beach route necessitated the reconstruction of several miles of long-neglected Southern Pacific track between Smeltzer and La Bolsa. This trackage, so busy during the oil boom of the 1920s, had fallen into disuse in the 1930s and had become covered in many places with silt and dirt. After assuming responsibility to operate this trackage in 1948, the P.E. at first handled only about six cars a day south of Stanton but business improved enough that the entire ten mile segment was rebuilt in the 1950s, using treated ties and heavier rail. Following this reconstruction the track was able to carry some fairly heavy loads. During the construction of Southern California Edison's power plant on the coast south of Huntington Beach in the late 1950s, some very heavy tonnage (primarily structural steel, cement and boiler components) were shipped via the Pacific Electric.

The P.E. bridge connecting Seal Beach with Long Beach was removed in 1958, finally severing the continuity of P.E.'s old Newport line. Subsequently, rail traffic declined along the remaining portion of coastal trackage, leading to the abandonment of the Huntington Beach-Newport track in 1962. The Huntington Beach-Seal Beach segment was removed in 1966, and the last two miles of former P.E. track in downtown Huntington Beach were lifted in 1976, but a cluster of lumber-oriented industries at the end of the remaining line (at old Wintersburg Station) still receive up to two daily visits by switching crews.

Another consolidation of operations over P.E. and S.P. freight trackage in Orange County came in 1955. Following the abandonment of the former electric interurban trackage on Fourth and Maple Streets in Santa Ana that year, P.E. obtained trackage rights over Espee trackage between Stanton and Dyer to serve the remnant of the old Santa Ana-Huntington Beach line between Dyer and Greenville (Costa Mesa). At the same time, additional rights enabled P.E. diesel switchers to run from Anaheim over to Marlboro to gain access to the Marlboro-Orange "island." As an alternate route into Orange County, the Pacific Electric was also given trackage rights over the Southern Pacific's line between Anaheim and Los Nietos, where P.E.'s Yorba Linda line crossed S.P.'s Puente Cut-off.

During the 1950s and early 1960s, the Pacific Electric did most of its freight work in Orange County with diesel locomotives leased from parent Southern Pacific, so, to the casual observer, it was difficult to tell where the operations of one company ended and those of the other began. This distinction ended in 1965 when Southern Pacific merged what was left of the entire P.E. system into its own system. Thereafter both companies' lines were considered S.P. property, although for some years following the merger labor agreements continued to reserve work in former P.E. territory for former P.E. crews.

The former Pacific Electric Yorba Linda line did not escape the paring-down process either. In 1963 P.E./S.P. and Union Pacific agreed to consolidate their parallel tracks between Colima, Laon Junction, and Fullerton, and to abandon the surplus trackage. The effect of this was to permit U.P. trains to use P.E.'s track between Colima and Laon, while P.E. (and later, successor S.P.) trains received trackage rights over the U.P. track from Laon to West Fullerton in order to serve the Hunt Foods complex. (Later, and until 1987, this trackage agreement was extended to permit S.P. trains to run over U.P. tracks as far as Anaheim.) In 1973 the former P.E. track to Yorba Linda was abandoned and removed back to a point called "Brea Chem," Union Oil's Brea facility at Kramer Avenue and Imperial Highway.

Although former Pacific Electric rail lines in Orange County have been severely cut back during the past four decades, other track abandonments have been relatively minor. Santa Fe's Olinda Spur was abandoned just prior to World War II although the wye track where the latter joined the main line at Richfield/Atwood remained in service until 1987. The Bastanchury Spur was lifted in the early 1950s, and Venta Spur, which served the Irvine Ranch, was abandoned in 1984, a victim of the growing urbanization of that part of the county.

In this beautifully proportioned, classic photograph, Santa Fe Pacific No. 3445 heads train No. 51, the San Bernadino to Los Angeles mail train, one mile west of Esperanza, in Santa Ana Canyon on April 14, 1951.
– Stan Kistler

To date the biggest loser on the Southern Pacific has been the Tustin Branch. It was cut back to Villa Park following the washout of the bridge over Santiago Creek in 1968 and in 1982 was further cut back to Marlboro. As of this writing, what remains of the line, including P.E.'s former "Orange island," survives on traffic to a number of light industrial plants. That portion of Southern Pacific's original rail line between West Anaheim and West Anaheim Junction was abandoned during the 1930s. The right of way eventually was deeded to the State of California for use in building the Santa Ana Freeway from Santa Ana Street to State College Boulevard; continuity of rail operations was assured by the retention of the downtown Anaheim "Loop Line" between these two points.

As this book went to press, an additional section of Southern Pacific's Santa Ana Branch was abandoned and surrendered in the name of freeway widening. The railroad trackage alongside the Santa Ana (I-5) Freeway between Katella Avenue in Anaheim and Seventeenth Street in Santa Ana has been removed to make way for more lanes on the freeway, and S.P. trains between these two points now travel over the Santa Fe, using trackage rights. Aside from the loss of this valuable rail right of way, this abandonment will result in the removal of the last Warren Truss bridge remaining in Orange County, and the obliteration of the historic, first rail crossing of the Santa Ana River in Orange County.

Two other former rail rights of way are now embedded in Orange County's freeway and highway network. The former Santa Ana & Newport Railway's right of way between Dyer and Newport is now occupied by the Costa Mesa (State Route 55) Freeway and Newport Boulevard. The tail end of S.P.'s former Tustin Branch, between Newport Boulevard and Browning Avenue, is now occupied by short sections of El Camino Real and Interstate 5.

The Changing Pattern of Passenger Operations

Passenger train operations in Orange County during the Twentieth Century present a far different pattern than those for freight. At the beginning of the century a total of five passenger trains made daily round trips between Los Angeles and Santa Ana, two via the Southern Pacific and three via the Santa

Both Southern Pacific and Union Pacific used McKeen-type gas-mechanical cars in local passenger service in Orange County, in an attempt to maintain convenient service at less cost. Although this picture of SP "windsplitter" No. 57 was taken in Los Angeles, the car was assigned to local service to Santa Ana as indicated by the train numbers it bears.
– Ed Kielty Collection

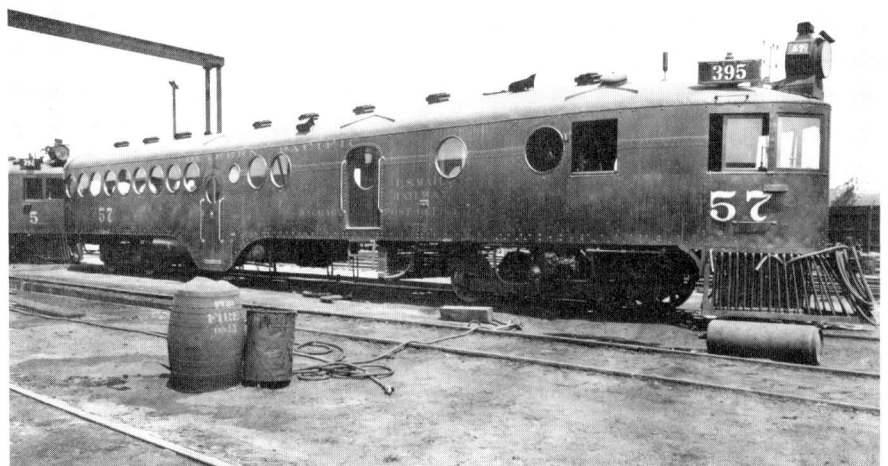

Fe (two of the latter running through to San Diego). The Santa Fe also ran one daily round trip from San Bernardino to Santa Ana and another between Los Angeles and San Bernardino, via Orange.

At this time the Southern Pacific also ran two trains a day over its Los Alamitos Branch, one train daily from Santa Ana to Newport (increased to two trains daily in summertime, and three on summer weekends), a single daily mixed (passenger and freight) train over the Tustin Branch, and three days per week (daily in winter) service from Newport to Smeltzer and back. These were all typical Espee branch line trains of the period: two to four wooden, open platform coaches pulled by a simple, saturated steam locomotive, usually either a 4-4-0 "American" or a 4-6-0 "Ten Wheeler." These trains usually travelled at between 20 and 25 miles per hour, which was not as leisurely as it seems in that pre-automobile era.

Between 1904 and 1907, as the newly arrived Pacific Electric was inaugurating faster, more frequent services to some Orange County communities, both the Santa Fe and the Southern Pacific responded with increased local passenger services of their own. Both railroads increased Los Angeles to Santa Ana round trips to three daily and the S.P. also increased service from Santa Ana to Newport to three daily trains (and even four trains during the summer of 1906). The Santa Fe added a third train from Los Angeles to San Diego in 1906 and a second train between Los Angeles and San Bernardino, via Orange, in 1909. Unable to compete effectively with P.E.'s electric trains, both S.P. and Santa Fe cut back their L.A. to Santa Ana local train services to former levels in 1908.

In 1910 the Santa Fe undertook significant improvements to its trackage in Orange County and passenger service improvements followed. New, heavier steel rail was laid between Los Angeles and San Diego, and the roadbed was reballasted and resurfaced. Just as important was the construction of the "Placentia Cut-off" between Fullerton and Richfield (Atwood). By eliminating the need for San Bernardino-bound trains to travel down to the wye junction at Orange, the rail journey between Fullerton and the Santa Ana Canyon line was shortened by eight miles. In 1911 the Santa Fe made good use of these improvements by increasing the number of L.A. to San Bernardino trains (via Orange County) to four daily round trips; at the same time L.A. to San Diego passenger service was increased to five daily round trips.

One of the new San Diego trains introduced at this time (1911) was named "The Saint" in one direction and "The Angel" in the other. Pulled by two new "high power" locomotives, the new trains catered to business and first class travel, having sleeping accommodations and two new "mission-style" parlor cars, and were extra fare only. In 1912 the runs of this famous duo of trains were extended to San Francisco (via Los Angeles, San Bernardino, Barstow and Mojave) and they became one of the Santa Fe's most famous California trains. Unfortunately, they were ordered discontinued by the United States Railroad Administration in 1918 as part of the Federal Government's rationalization of regional passenger services.

By 1913 all day trains on the L.A. to San Diego run through Orange County had a parlor observation car and all night trains had sleeping accommodations. Pre-Amtrak services on Santa Fe's "Surf Line" to San Diego peaked at seven daily round trips in 1915, when Trains 70 and 77 were put on to accommodate increased traffic to the Panama-California Exposition in San Diego. These trains were discontinued in 1917 following the close of the fair.

While the Santa Fe was improving service on its longer lines through Orange County, the Southern Pacific continued to seek a means to provide better service at an economical operating cost on its network of short local branch lines. Orange County residents were given a vision of the future when a "McKeen" gasoline-mechanical car toured the Southern Pacific in a western states promotional junket in 1906. The new car, manufactured in Omaha by the McKeen Corporation, in close cooperation with the Harriman management of U.P. and S.P., was more economical to operate than a conventional branch line steam train. It displayed unique "streamlined," or "windsplitter," contours, and was fitted with porthole-type windows. Each car seated about 60 passengers and offered heating, drinking water, and toilets (the last not usually available to electric interurban passengers in those days).

The McKeen car was widely touted as being the steam railroads' response to the competitive threat posed by interurban trolley cars, and rumors flew through the local press as to where they would be used in Southern California. In fact, the Southern Pacific did not purchase McKeens for its own use until 1908 and, despite petitions from local citizens, did not have enough to deploy any south of the Tehachapis until 1910. In January of that year one McKeen finally began handling local traffic on the Southern Pacific over a route from the city of San Fernando on the north via Los Angeles (Arcade Station) to Santa Ana. One year later (in January of 1911) the McKeen car's run was extended south to Newport, displacing the last non-mixed steam passenger service to that point.

On August 16, 1947, the second eastbound section of Santa Fe Train No. 24, the "Grand Canyon," passes Basta Tower and the crossing of Commonwealth Avenue in western Fullerton. The interlocking tower protected the crossing with Union Pacific's Anaheim Branch.
– Ralph Melching

Ironically, by 1912 the Southern Pacific was engaged in hauling cement and concrete aggregate over the line between Santa Ana and Newport to facilitate the construction of the first paved highway between those two points. After the highway was finished motor bus competition was established which contributed to the elimination of McKeen service south of Santa Ana in 1914. At the same time this cutback was implemented in January of 1914, the S. P.

doubled the number of McKeen trips between Los Angeles and Santa Ana. With this addition there was now a total of four daily round trip passenger trains on the branch, two of them steam powered and the other two McKeen cars.

The overall frequency of Southern Pacific passenger service in Orange County had begun to decline by 1915 as that company took advantage of its full ownership of the Pacific Electric to coordinate certain services (see Chapter 4). Where S.P. and P.E. provided passenger service to the same points, ticket agents were encouraged to use the electric trains rather than steam locals. In some cases passenger services were relegated almost in their entirety to the P.E. In 1916 Southern Pacific discontinued the last two remaining steam-powered passenger trains between Los Angeles and Santa Ana, leaving only the two daily round trips provided by McKeen cars.

Attempts by the United States Railroad Administration to rationalize the county's passenger services during 1918 brought further cutbacks. Federal managers adjusted local schedules to divert L.A.-Santa Ana patrons to either the Pacific Electric (which was not under federal control) or the Santa Fe, and the Southern Pacific's two motor trains were cut back to terminate in Anaheim instead of Santa Ana. After the war the S.P. found that revenues from the Anaheim McKeen cars covered only one third of operating expenses and sought their discontinuance in 1921. Two years later, on August 12, 1923, the California Railroad Commission granted permission for the Southern Pacific to discontinue its McKeen service to Anaheim. At the same time the "Merry-Go-Round Mixed" train (see Chapter 5) was also removed from the timetable. These actions brought an end to Southern Pacific's remaining local passenger and mixed services in Orange County.

Just as the Southern Pacific was preparing to end its passenger services in the county, another major railroad began operating a new local passenger service, also using the ubiquitous McKeen car. The newcomer was the Union Pacific, which opened its branch to Anaheim on July 1, 1923 (see Chapter 5).

In a scene reminiscent of the 1930s, Northern No. 3758 leads an unidentified eastbound, all-heavyweight train crossing Highland Avenue in Fullerton in 1952.
– Stan Kistler

U.P. offered two daily round trips from Anaheim to Pico (Whittier) Junction and to Los Angeles. Connections were offered to eastbound and westbound main line trains. During the six weeks between the commencement of U.P.'s service and the discontinuance of Espee's, Anaheim boasted of four daily round trip motor trains to Los Angeles, in addition to the main line services on the Santa Fe Railway!

The Union Pacific passenger service was apparently no more successful than had been the Southern Pacific's. U.P.'s McKeens did not attract sufficient patronage to justify their expense, and in 1927 the railroad asked the State

The popularity of the San Diegan service is shown by this view of Santa Fe's famous E1 diesel No. 4 heading a twelve-car first section of the northbound "San Diegan" at Gallivan, near today's Oso Parkway in Mission Viejo, August 18, 1951.
– Stan Kistler

Railroad Commission for permission to replace them with busses. The discontinuance of local passenger service on the Anaheim Branch did not happen easily, however.

Hearings conducted during 1927 found that an average of four passengers a day rode the motor trains, of which 75 percent made use of the transcontinental connections and the other 25 percent were making purely local journeys along the branch itself or to Los Angeles. Union Pacific proposed to substitute motor busses for these trains, to be operated by a subsidiary, Union Pacific Stage Company. In a potentially landmark case, the Commission granted permission to discontinue the trains but denied authority to operate a bus service. The Commission found that Motor Transit Company (then an

A "sideswipe" collision between a steam-hauled passenger local and a diesel-powered "San Diegan" occurred on the west switch of the Orange wye on April 18, 1942. This view of the accident shows 1909-vintage Atlantic (4-4-2) No. 1468 in the ditch. This train had come down the Olive District from San Bernardino, stopped at Orange, then backed up and was occupying the north-to-west leg of the wye in order to run up to Fullerton and Los Angeles. Unfortunately, the engineer of this train mistakenly occupied the junction switch just as a northbound "San Diegan" came through.
– K.L. Post photo, George Leichtfus Collection

This view of the 1942 Orange Junction wreck shows El diesel unit No. 3-3A in the dirt on the south side of the right of way. Although both trains were packed with wartime riders, and there were some injuries, fortunately no one was killed. While the accident tied up the junction, San Diego corridor trains had to be rerouted via Atwood and the Olive District.
– K.L. Post photo, George Leichtfus Collection

independent operator) had "twenty auto stages daily each way in close proximity to the stations proposed to be served by the Union Pacific Stage Company." Since Motor Transit offered to adjust its routes to accommodate U.P. passengers, and because it offered a slightly lower tariff, the Commission gave Motor Transit permission to operate the replacement service. Interestingly, in addition to expressing concern that U.P. Stages was an interstate carrier over which it would have no jurisdiction, the Commission found that "burdening the highways with an additional stage line to transport [a] negligible amount of passengers" was unjustifiable.

This decision was handed down in December of 1927 but it was not the final word. Six months later the Commission revoked the decision, requiring the passenger train service to continue. Not until May 15, 1929 did the McKeen trains cease running over the Anaheim branch. Although U.P. Stages began operating a connecting bus service between U.P.'s East Los Angeles

In 1952, two nearly new Budd-built rail diesel cars in "San Diegan" service hustle south through the orange groves just north of San Juan Capistrano.
– Stan Kistler

Still new Budd RDC's in "San Diegan" service, southbound to San Diego in this 1952 view taken at San Clemente, whisk past Santa Fe's old depot which had been closed for nearly 15 years.
– Stan Kistler

depot and Anaheim on that date, it was not until August of 1930 that the stage line finally obtained state commission approval for the service.

Despite the discontinuance of local passenger operations in Orange County by two of the main line railroad companies, the third carrier — Santa Fe — continued to provide a high level of service on its through trains. On Santa Fe's San Diego line, service during the 1920s and 1930s continued at just

Although modernized with lightweight "streamliner" cars in the late 1930s, not all of the "San Diegan" passenger trains were diesel-powered until the early 1950s. Here, Northern No. 3758 easily pulls a southbound "San Diegan" through San Clemente in 1951.
— Stan Kistler

below pre-war levels with four round trips daily. These trains featured all-steel Pullmans on the one night train and parlor cars on the three daytime runs.

Passenger service from Los Angeles to San Bernardino via Orange County dropped from five trains a day during World War I to between two and 3 1/2 in the 1920s and 1930s. This service was a combination of transcontinental trains and local services. The fractional number of round trips at certain times resulted from some trains running one way via the Third District, and returning over the Second District via Pasadena and the San Gabriel Valley. Santa Fe's interstate "name trains" which operated on the Third District through Santa Ana Canyon and northern Orange County during these decades included "The Missionary," "The Fargo Fast," "The Phoenix," "The Scout," "The Santa Fe Eight," "The Fast Mail," and "The Grand Canyon."

Not long after Union Pacific discontinued its motor trains into Orange County, the Santa Fe introduced a new generation of motor trains on some of its

Santa Fe's last steam-powered heavyweight trains to operate in the Orange County-San Diego corridor were local all-stops mail and express Trains 70 and 75. This 1951 view shows the northbound train, powered by Mountain No. 3741, pausing at Santa Ana to conduct some head end business.
– Marshall Nelson

Santa Fe F-units Nos. 168A & B head a northbound local train made up of six heavyweight cars, just north of the pier at San Clemente, August 18, 1951.
– Stan Kistler

lines. In 1930, in conjunction with a reduction in services between Los Angeles and San Bernardino, Santa Fe began running new Electro-Motive Corporation gas-electric motor cars. Far more efficient and mechanically reliable than their McKeen cousins, the EMC motor trains likewise saved the expense of a conventional steam-powered train. The locals were variously routed through northern Orange County: sometimes they ran via the Placentia Cut-off and sometimes on the older, longer route via Anaheim, Orange, and Olive. The motor trains offered a convenient accommodation service in the mostly rural territory they traversed; they could be flagged at every little crossroads station along the route and they carried express parcels and the U.S. Mails, too. Surprisingly, patronage on these trains seems to have increased enough in the late 1930s and during the 1940s so that conventional steam trains were often required to handle the business. These accommodation trains were given Santa Fe train numbers in the "50" series, and the last one was discontinued in 1955.

Nineteen thirty eight was a watershed year for Santa Fe passenger service through Orange County, for it was in March that streamlined, diesel-powered "San Diegan" service was inaugurated. These trains were part of an overall upgrade in passenger service undertaken by the Santa Fe which included both train modernization and a co-ordinated rail and bus transportation concept covering the principle markets in the state of California. Speed and comfort were improved while rates were reduced 25 percent to an average of only 1 1/2 cents per mile. The fare from Santa Ana to San Francisco, for example, was reduced to $6.50. The fare from Santa Ana to San Diego was reduced to $1.31 and the already low weekend round trip rate of $2.00 was retained. Although the new "Super Chief" and "El Capitan" paid promotional visits to Orange County in 1938, they did not enter Orange County on their regular runs; the San Diegans were the county's first taste of modern streamlined rail travel.

A second set of San Diegan equipment was added in 1941, and a lunch counter diner and round-end observation lounge were added to each trainset. With the addition of this new equipment, train frequency increased to five round trips daily. Four of these trains were entitled to wear the distinctive "San Diegan" drumhead, and one train, composed of conventional heavyweight rolling stock, was retained to accommodate local (flagstop) passengers and express business. Scheduled service on the "Surf Line" continued at this level for the next decade although numerous extra sections and extra trains were run during the Second World War.

The number of daily trains to and from San Diego was increased to six in 1952 when two self-propelled Budd-built rail diesel cars were introduced to this corridor. The scheduled frequency of trains once again matched the all-time Santa Fe high (of 1915-17) when a seventh round trip was added in 1954, but this dropped back to six in 1956 when the rail diesel cars were taken off following a wreck at Redondo Junction in Los Angeles. Eight years later, even though 700 Orange County passengers used the Santa Fe corridor services daily, the end of the mail contract resulted in a reduction to only four round trips each day. In 1965, the Santa Fe eliminated commute-hour passenger service, cutting back to three trains daily on the San Diego line. Accompanying this reduction in service, the total number of passengers carried by the Santa Fe between Los Angeles and San Diego declined from 1 million in 1947 to 500,000 in the early 1960s. In the 1960s, about half the passengers using the "San Diegans" travelled to or from Orange County stations.

The Santa Ana Canyon route suffered even greater losses. After the discontinuance of "The Fast Mail" in 1965, only the "Grand Canyon" used that route over the eastern end of the Third District. In 1968 this train was rerouted

On January 19, 1968, an abbreviated "Grand Canyon" heads into upper Santa Ana Canyon. On the other side of the bridge the train will cross into Orange County on the last leg of its westbound journey from Chicago. Santa Fe's once-famous Train No. 23, shorn of its vital mail contract, will soon fade into history. Prado Dam is to the right of the photograph area.
– T.M. Hotchkiss photo, William A. Myers Collection

via Pasadena, ending passenger service over Santa Fe's original route into Orange County.

The National Railroad Passenger Corporation, better known as Amtrak, took over all the surviving rail passenger services in Orange County (and virtually everywhere else in the nation) on May 1, 1971. There followed a period when passenger equipment from many different carriers could be found on the trains travelling through the county as Amtrak consolidated the fleet of cars inherited from the predecessor rail carriers. (Not surprisingly, Santa Fe's passenger cars and locomotives were generally found to be in the best condition, and virtually its entire fleet was taken over by Amtrak.) In the mid-1970s, Amtrak began introducing its standardized "Amfleet" coach and club car designs on the L.A. to San Diego corridor, and the older "streamlined" cars soon disappeared.

In the first year of Amtrak operation there was even a through car attached to one of the three daily San Diegans, which, three days a week, travelled north via the "Coast Starlight" to the Bay Area, Portland and Seattle. Although this was a relatively short-lived experiment, it did demonstrate the fact that the rail corridor which served Orange County communities did not have to end arbitrarily at Union Station in Los Angeles.

Thanks to increasing patronage and financial support from various levels of government, frequency of passenger train service on the busy corridor through Orange County has increased to a new all-time high. In fact, by the late 1970s the Los Angeles to San Diego route had become the second busiest Amtrak route in the United States! Reflecting this growth in demand for service, a fourth round trip was restored in 1976, a fifth in 1977, and a sixth in 1978, all in response to the growing population in Southern California along the Santa Fe/Amtrak corridor, to the motor fuel shortages of the 1970s, and to increased highway congestion. A seventh round trip was added in 1980, matching the highest frequencies ever offered by the Santa Fe (in 1915-17 and 1954-56). Services were further increased in 1987 by the introduction of an eighth daily round trip. At the same time, all passenger services in this corridor were revolutionized by the start of push-pull operations which cut down on the servicing times required at each end of the run. In 1988 one round trip daily was extended to a new northern terminus in Santa Barbara, again demonstrating that Southern California's transportation needs do not have to be constrained by historic boundaries between the old operating companies. Service through Santa Ana Canyon returned in 1986 when Amtrak rerouted its Superliner-equipped "Desert Wind," which runs between Los Angeles and Salt Lake City.

This renovation extends to the infrastructure too. Santa Fe's Fullerton depot is the last of the old depots in Orange County which continues to serve rail travellers, although San Juan Capistrano depot, now a restaurant, does still function as a passenger stop. In addition, two new facilities have been built. The City of Anaheim constructed a small station adjacent to Anaheim Stadium, and in 1985 the City of Santa Ana opened its impressive Regional Transportation Center north of the old Santa Fe station which was subsequently demolished. A third new station opened in 1990 to serve Irvine and El Toro.

Track on the corridor through Orange County has been maintained to Santa Fe's traditionally high standards, and speeds up to 90 miles per hour are routinely achieved, especially in the southern portion of the county. During 1988 the track between Fullerton and South Santa Ana was rebuilt; this, along with the planned addition of sections of double track, will increase the capacity of the route.

During the past two and a half decades, Amtrak patronage on the lines through Orange County has climbed steadily. Ridership on the San Diego line has substantially exceeded 150,000 patrons *each month* for the past two years and is still rising, putting to rest the myth that Southern Californians cannot be wooed away from their automobiles. Many Orange County residents, and there are now three million of them, use the service to commute to work (both inside and outside the county), as well as to make connections with transcontinental trains in Los Angeles. As this book was written a task force was reviewing plans for further additions to local passenger services in the county. Clearly, the decade of the 1980s has seen the Santa Fe rail corridor through Orange County become one of the major rail passenger routes in the nation, with a potential for even greater levels of service in the near future.

Excursions and Specials

In addition to the regularly scheduled passenger services in the county, there have been, over the years, a number of excursions and other special movements. Even before the Santa Fe line through the county was completed, it was carrying crowds of excursionists to the ocean shore (see Chapter 2). Summer holiday excursions to the beach over the Santa Ana & Newport were popular in the 1890s and early 1900s. Special fraternal conventions and other public events also drew large crowds who travelled by rail.

When "The Great White Fleet" cruised up the coast on the Pacific leg of its circumnavigation of the world, special trains carried people to coastal sites to view the ships as they passed by offshore. Both Santa Fe and Pacific Electric operated special trains each New Years Day to carry people to Pasadena for the Rose Parade, and from the mid-Twenties the football game as well. The 1915 Panama-California Exposition in San Diego rated a pair of trains on the Santa Fe as was mentioned earlier in this chapter. The Southern Pacific once sponsored seasonal excursions to Orange County for its own employees. These specials consisted of as many as four entire trains which ran from Los Angeles to the Orange Coast. The last such excursion was operated in 1928, five years after the Espee had discontinued regular passenger service in the county.

After the Del Mar Race Track began operation north of San Diego in 1937, during each race season the Santa Fe ran many extras and race track specials directly to sidings beside the race track for the convenience of patrons. This seasonal special service continued at least until the summer of 1968. From

The Railroad Boosters, now known as the Pacific Railroad Society, chartered a train of heavyweight passenger equipment for an excursion of Santa Fe's Orange County trackage in 1939. Here the train pauses at the Orange depot.
– Ralph Melching

the late 1930s special trips were chartered for railroad enthusiasts; in the late 1940s and early 1950s these trips often included travel on remote freight-only branches of all four of the county's rail carriers.

To celebrate Orange County's prosperity, one year an entire group of businessmen from around the nation — all delegates to the national convention

The Union Pacific's Anaheim Branch was finally built in 1923. Thirty three years later, the last steam powered rail enthusiast excursion into Orange County was held on June 9, 1956, when Union Pacific 0-6-0 switcher No. 4456 and a train consisting of ex-Los Angeles Terminal Railway wooden coaches travelled down the Anaheim Branch. This view shows the excursion train in the Friendly Hills section of Fullerton, near Las Palmas Drive.
— Jack Hedden photo, Mark Effle Collection

The 1956 excursion also stopped at the Fullerton station. This building has been preserved and now houses a restaurant adjacent to Fullerton's Amtrak (ex-Santa Fe) depot.
— Jack Hedden photo, Mark Effle Collection

of the Chamber of Commerce — arrived in the county aboard the Santa Fe and were treated to the hospitality of Santa Ana and the Irvine Ranch. On another occasion, Santa Fe President Fred Gurley served a special dinner in the county prepared by the famed Fred Harvey dining department in honor of one of the county's leading ranchers.

Probably the greatest single special railroad movement into Orange County occurred in 1953. Seventy special passenger trains brought 50,000 Boy Scouts from all over the world to an international Jamboree held on the grounds of the Irvine Ranch. (Jamboree Road in Newport Beach commemorates this event.) Thirty five of these trains came directly into the county over the Santa Fe. Passengers on the other 35 trains debarked at S.P.'s Walnut Station and were bussed to the Jamboree site. The event was capped, from the railroad's viewpoint, by a reenactment of the driving of the Golden Spike at the Jamboree site. This activity used two nineteenth century steam locomotives and some old trackage borrowed from Hollywood movie studios, all of which had to be trucked in to the (then) remote site on a hill on the ranch overlooking Upper Newport Bay. (Coincidently, twenty five years later, not far from the site of this reenactment, Costa Mesa's O'Connor Engineering Company constructed the two full-sized replica locomotives now operated by the National Park Service at the Golden Spike National Historic Site in Utah.)

Conclusion

It has been more than a hundred years since the first railroad track was built into what became Orange County. Railroads were the first major industry (other than agriculture) in the county, and in all the years which followed the railroads played an important, often pivotal part in its economic development. Over the years there have been many changes in the technology and operating procedures employed by the railroads, yet bits of the past's rich heritage have been preserved. The steam locomotive era which ended on the county's main line railroads in the early 1950s has been kept alive by the county's world-class theme parks. Knott's Berry Farm has preserved a fine stable of authentic 1880s-era narrow gauge equipment from Colorado, and Disneyland operates a beautifully-maintained narrow gauge railroad using replicas of nineteenth-century equipment built in the 1950s. Together the railroads at these two tourist parks run up more passenger-miles annually than many more famous tourist railroads across the country.

Despite the changes of the past several decades and despite changes in market orientation as well, Orange County's railroads remain dynamic and viable, even given the changing economic conditions of the late 1980s. In addition to the growth in passenger traffic described previously, freight traffic handled by the county's three rail carriers generates a daily average approaching 200 rail cars, and a dozen different crews are required to service all of the line-side customers. Admittedly, most of the former freight depots have been closed, and some trackage removed but new spurs and sidings are still being added each year within the county. In addition, railroad-owned real estate continues to play an important role in the county's development. The railroads, which have been so important to the history of Orange County, are partners in the county's present and will be a part of its future as well.

Train No. 7, Santa Fe's "Fast Mail and Express", races into Atwood, California on the Third District of the Los Angeles Division circa 1963. The train was traveling at the maximum authorized speed of 79 mph. A deserted Orangethorpe Boulevard and surrounding groves are markedly different from today's urban clutter.
— Painting by John Signor

Late on the afternoon of August 27, 1970, Cliff Prather created a fascinating silhouette of milling passengers and well-wishers against the reflecting sun on the fluted stainless steel of the northbound "San Diegan" at Fullerton.
— C.R. Prather

7 Color Cornucopia

Rail Photography in the Orange Groves

Since the advent of color photography in the late 1930's, rail photographers have enjoyed much expanded opportunity to capture the beauty and excitment of Orange County railroading on film. The photographs included here have been chosen to illustrate many of the locations described in earlier chapters, inhabited as they were by the area's four railroads — Pacific Electric, Santa Fe, Southern Pacific, and Union Pacific — and to reflect the rich geographical diversity of Orange County with its broad spectrum of vistas, from densely populated urban settings to the peacefulness of rural countryside.

243

Color pictures of Pacific Electric trolley cars in Orange County are rare, but famed rail historian Donald Duke captured the essence of "Red Car" service to Southern California in this beautiful view of interurban car No. 1044 southbound on the beach-hugging Newport line, just south of Huntington Beach, on October 30, 1949. The occasion was a rail enthusiast excursion over this soon-to-be-abandoned line.
– Donald Duke Photo, Tom Gildersleeve Collection

In 1940, SP Consolidation No. 2554 hit a truck carrying bees at the intersection of Wanda and Collins Avenues on the Tustin Branch. Before the steam locomotive could be rerailed, angry bees had to be dispersed by smoke, and SP crews had to borrow a Union Pacific crane.
– Weldon Field

Santa Fe Northern No. 3758 awaits the conductor's signal to depart Santa Ana on its northbound journey to Los Angeles, July 12, 1951. Some of the passengers boarding here may transfer to "The Chief" at Los Angeles Union Passenger Terminal. Orange County's status as the nation's premier citrus-growing region is shown by the giant Treesweet juice plant behind the train.
– Tom Gildersleeve

Santa Fe Mikado No. 3256 thunders southbound through orange groves west of Fullerton with a local freight, circa 1950.
–Marshall Nelson

A southbound "San Diegan" skirts the surf along the bluffs just south of San Clemente, seconds from the south boundary of Orange County in the late afternoon of July 4, 1964.
– Tom Gildersleeve

A pair of Santa Fe Budd "Rail Diesel Cars" crosses Fourth Street in Santa Ana in June 1958, having just departed the Santa Ana depot on their northbound journey to Los Angeles. For several years in the mid-1950s, these RDCs ran in "San Diegan" service until a tragic wreck at Redondo Junction caused the Santa Fe to return to traditional locomotive and coach consists.
– Tom Gildersleeve

By 1951, Santa Fe was using utilitarian GP9 road switchers to haul some of its lesser passenger services. This northbound local mail train rounds the big curve just south of Santa Ana on July 12th.
– Tom Gildersleeve

This fine view of a warbonnet-liveried "San Diegan" northbound at Irvine Station (later Valencia) was taken on July 5, 1964, and is representative of Santa Fe passenger services through Orange County in the last decade of the pre-Amtrak era.
– Tom Gildersleeve

Deep in what is now the Orange County community of Mission Viejo, a northbound Santa Fe "San Diegan" makes its way through grassy rolling hills of still rural ranch land in this May 23, 1964 view. The streamliner has just passed under the bridge carrying U.S. 101 (now I-5) over the railroad.
– Tom Gildersleeve

A year before Amtrak was to take over all passenger rail service in Orange County, Santa Fe's "San Diegan" pauses at the Santa Ana depot on its way northbound to Los Angeles, in April 1970. This station served until 1985, when it was replaced by the new Transportation Center.
— Jim Walker

The first train into the new Santa Ana Regional Transportation Center, Amtrak No. 571, the "San Diegan" is seen here on a rainy September 4, 1985.
— C.R. Prather

Santa Fe Train No. 75, a "San Diegan," is northbound on a hot, sultry afternoon in May, 1970 as the heat rises visibly in waves from the baking acreage.
– C.R. Prather

Amtrak No. 770, the "San Diegan" heads into the siding eastbound at Valencia, in October of 1977.
— Jim Minor

The yellow-and-black striped control cab of Amtrak's "push-pull" San Diegan corridor service burnishes Santa Fe rails through one of the last orange groves remaining on the Irvine Ranch in November, 1987.
– Jim Minor

249

Southern Pacific Switcher No. 1205 pulls a
string of beet gons at Santa Ana on June
18, 1976. Note the unusual track
configuration: the track under the train
courses back in the distance to cross the track
in the foreground.
— C.R. Prather

Heavy mainline power dominates auto
traffic on Olive Street in downtown
Anaheim on February 12, 1984. SP's
"Hauler" is heading to South Anaheim and
a return to the private right of way along
the Santa Ana Freeway (I-5).
— C.R. Prather

Holly Sugar 1, which is seen here at Dyer on the SP on January 19, 1980, was built in 1939 by the Electro-Motive Corporation, forerunner to today's locomotive giant EMD, part of General Motors. This locomotive played a significant role in Southern Pacific history, being the railroad's first diesel-powered locomotive, No. 1000.
— Dick Stephenson

Southern Pacific No. 1178 heads north across Fifth Street in West Santa Ana on former Pacific Electric trackage on February 12, 1972.
– C.R. Prather

SP No. 3366 switches cars at the Union Oil Refinery at "Brea Chem" on September 30, 1986. Since 1968, this has been the end of track on the former Pacific Electric Yorba Linda line.
– C.R. Prather

On April 27, 1986, passenger service returned to the Santa Ana Canyon trackage with the rerouting of Amtrak's "Desert Wind" between Los Angeles and Salt Lake City. Six days later on May 3 a westbound passes the old Bryant Ranch east of Horseshoe Curve.
— William A. Myers

A four-unit Santa Fe diesel leads a westbound freight around the curve east of Esperanza early on the morning of December 20, 1986. Units one and four are in the short-lived paint scheme which anticipated a merger between the Santa Fe and the Southern Pacific which was denied ICC approval.
— Jim Minor

252

The Olive District of the Santa Fe is still an important route for freight trains running between San Bernardino and San Diego. In this March 26, 1972 view, the southbound San Diego local passes an abandoned Sunkist citrus packing house at the site of the old Olive depot.
— C.R. Prather

The trains continue to roll as Orange County develops more and more of its land into housing tracts and business and retail centers. Here, Amtrak No. 35, the "Desert Wind," heads towards Los Angeles at Esperanza (in Santa Ana Canyon) after being rerouted due to a problem on the Santa Fe's First Subdivision (through Pasadena) on March 5, 1983. Today, the "Desert Wind" has been permanently rerouted through Orange County, making this once-unusual scene commonplace.
— C.R. Prather

A northbound Santa Fe freight passes milepost 37.5 at the east end of Horseshoe Curve in Santa Ana Canyon in November of 1987.
– Jim Daily

253

Southern Pacific's historic Warren Truss bridge over the Santa Ana River vibrates to heavy tonnage for the last time on February 9, 1988. This was the last southbound train to cross this bridge, which was removed from service to facilitate the widening of the adjacent freeway.
— Terry Wegmann

The SP Costa Mesa local freight pulls past the Anaheim Stadium station as it exercises its trackage rights on the Santa Fe. The crowded nature of recent building in the area is in stark contrast to its former rural character. The man kneeling on the platform with two children is yet another reminder of the magnetic attraction so many of us have with trains.
— C.R. Prather

A clear January 20, 1990 finds the SP Costa Mesa local heading south at Greenville, between freshly tilled fields and housing subdivisions — truly an Orange County vista — with a backdrop of the San Gabriel Mountains towering above the scene.
— C.R. Prather

254

UP 3093 on the point of the Anaheim local freight at Sunny Hills on August 22, 1987. Appropriately, the name of the location is reflected in the bright, primary colors captured in the photograph.
— C.R. Prather

Mid-day on May 18, 1985 finds the Union Pacific's Anaheim local trundling back towards La Habra after making a trip out on the Anaheim branch. The old Pacific Electric Fullerton branch roadbed and bridge can be seen above the train.
— C.R. Prather

A Northbound UP local freight crosses Santa Fe's main line at Basta Tower, just west of Fullerton, on May 18, 1985.
— C.R. Prather

Disneyland Railroad No. 4, "Ernest S. Marsh," at Main Street Station, circa 1980.
– © The Walt Disney Company

A Appendix
Orange County's Amusement Park Railroads

In addition to its network of common carrier railroads, Orange County also enjoys the services of two narrow gauge amusement park rail lines, at Disneyland and Knott's Berry Farm, respectively. These two railroads are among the busiest rail passenger carriers in the nation, together accounting for most of the nation's remaining narrow gauge steam train passenger mileage.

Disneyland

At the age of 16, Walt Disney worked as a news butcher (a seller of newspapers, magazines, candy and soft drinks) on Santa Fe trains running between Kansas City and Jefferson City, Missouri. The creator of Mickey Mouse and other cartoon characters later built a one-eighth full size (inch and a half to the foot scale) live steam railroad around the grounds of his Southern California home. Trains on this oversized model railroad were pulled by an 1890s-era 4-4-0 "American" type locomotive named "Lilly Belle" which Disney built himself. There are some who claim it was this model railroad that first gave Disney the idea for a theme park.

When Disney's amusement park was being built in orange groves south of the Orange County city of Anaheim, a mile and a half-long railroad was laid out to encircle the park. The scale of the ride was determined in typical Disney fashion. "Imagineers" built a plywood "mockup" of the proposed train. When it was determined that a six-foot doorway was just large enough for a human passenger to walk through, the remainder of the train was constructed proportionately. All of this led to the selection of a gauge of three feet for the rails.

Disney used his little "Lilly Belle" as the prototype for the first two steam locomotives built for the amusement park. Design work, pattern-making, and detail work was done by the Walt Disney Studios in Burbank. Wheels, frames, boilers, cylinders, and drive gear were cast, finished, and assembled by O'Connor Engineering of Costa Mesa whose owner, Chad O'Connor, was a fellow steam enthusiast. Final assembly and finish painting of the diminutive locomotives was done at the square "roundhouse" at Disneyland. The resulting locomotives were authentic replicas in every detail of the type of steam locomotives used on American railroads during the late nineteenth century.

Walt Disney shared the initial cost of building his theme park with corporate co-sponsors who underwrote part of the construction and maintenance costs of specific rides, in exchange for having their name associated with that

Table A.1:
Locomotives of the Disneyland Railroad
(Formerly the Santa Fe and Disneyland Railroad)

(All equipment is 36-inch gauge)

No.	Name	Wheel Type	Builder	Date	Number	Note
1	C. K. Holliday	4-4-0	Disney	1955	n/a	(1)
2	E. P. Ripley	4-4-0	Disney	1955	n/a	(2)
3	Fred Gurley	2-4-4	Baldwin	1895	14065	(3)
4	Ernest S. Marsh	2-4-4	Baldwin	1925	58367	(4)

Notes:

(1)   Boiler and running gear built by O'Connor Engineering; erection and finish work done by Walt Disney Studios (1955); Santa Fe and Disneyland Railroad No. 1 (1955); renamed Disneyland Railroad No. 1 (10-1974); in service 1988.

(2)   Boiler and running gear built by O'Connor Engineering; erection and finish work done by Walt Disney Studios (1955); Santa Fe and Disneyland Railroad No. 2 (1955); renamed Disneyland Railroad No. 2 (10-1974); in service 1988.

(3)   Built as 0-4-4T, wood burner (1895); La Fourche, Raceland & Longport Railway No. 1 (1895); converted to coal burner (c. 1922) sold to Georgia Plantation, Mathews, Louisiana (1951); sold to C.W. Witbeck, Hammond, Louisiana (1956); sold to Walt Disney (1958); extensively rebuilt, converted to 2-4-4 oil burner (1958); Santa Fe and Disneyland Railroad No. 3 (1958); renamed Disneyland Railroad No. 3 (10-1974); in service 1988.

(4)   Built as 0-4-4 Forney type, wood burner (1925); original owner and number unknown (date unknown); sold to Walt Disney (1958); extensively rebuilt, converted to 2-4-4 oil burner (1958-9); Santa Fe and Disneyland Railroad No. 4 (1959); renamed Disneyland Railroad No. 4 (10-1974); in service 1988.

(Source: Walt Disney Archives; Butler, W.E. *Down Among the Sugar Cane*)

ride. The steam train ride around the park was co-sponsored by the Atchison, Topeka and Santa Fe Railway, and was originally called the "Santa Fe and Disneyland Railroad." The first two 4-4-0 locomotives were named after early Santa Fe presidents. Locomotive No. 1 bore the name "C.K. Holliday," and Locomotive No. 2 became the "E.P. Ripley." Walt Disney was at the throttle of the "Holliday" for the first trip around Disneyland on opening day in 1955.

The ride proved to be very popular, perhaps in part due to the fact that these little steamers went to work just as the last steam locomotives disappeared from the main line railroads in Southern California. Three years after Disneyland opened it became necessary to obtain two more locomotives to accomodate increased patronage. Because the 4-4-0 wheel arrangement did not provide sufficient tractive effort for the heavy train loads of patrons carried each day on the railroad, Disney engineers took a different path in the search for "new" steam engines. Rather than build new locomotives from the wheels up, Disney sought the help of long-time friend and locomotive historian Gerald M. Best to find two suitable candidates from among the few preserved steam locomotives remaining in the United States.

Best located two small 0-4-4 Forney-type locomotives which had been used on industrial railroads. One had been built in 1895 for a sugar plantation near New Orleans, and the other had been built in 1925 for a lumber mill in New England. Both fit the bill for tractive power, gauge, appearance and general condition. They were shipped to Southern California and thoroughly reconstructed, in the process becoming oil-fired, 2-4-4 locomotives. The former sugar cane engine entered service in 1958 as Locomotive No. 3, "Fred Gurley," named for the then-current Chairman of the Santa Fe. A year later, the former New England lumber hauler appeared as Locomotive No. 4, "Ernest S. Marsh," named for Santa Fe's President.

In addition to these historic steam locomotives, Disneyland also has four complete trains of rolling stock. The "Holiday Special" is a train composed of three cattle cars, four gondolas, and a caboose. One train is an "excursion train" made up of replicas of so-called "Narragansett" cars, a roofed, open-sided design once used on summer-time excursion trains in New England. Two trains feature side seating, facing inwards toward the park. There is also an ornate parlor car, the "Lilly Belle," a special car reserved for the use of invited guests.

Walt Disney, himself a railroad enthusiast, enjoyed driving a steam locomotive on the opening day of his new Disneyland theme park, June 28, 1955.
– © The Walt Disney Company

Former Denver & Rio Grande No. 41 as it
appeared in service at Knott's Berry Farm,
circa 1980. This short-lived paint scheme
was replaced by a more authentic replica of
that used during its service on the Rio
Grande Southern.
– Knott's Berry Farm

All the rolling stock was designed by WED Enterprises and was built at Walt Disney Studios.

In October of 1974, all of the park's steam locomotives and rolling stock were repainted with the name "Disneyland Railroad." This reflected the ending of a long relationship with the Santa Fe Railway. The locomotives have kept their original names, however.

The 3-foot narrow gauge railroad around the park is old-fashioned in appearance only, for it is protected by automatic block signals, crossing gates and warning lights. Each locomotive and train is carefully cleaned, washed and polished every night after the park closes, in preparation for the next day's visitors. If necessary, the daily maintenance may include touching up the paint, so that the equipment always looks brand new. The locomotives are rotated in service, so that three are "on call" for use, and the fourth is in the backshop for a heavy overhaul. This level of maintenance is in keeping with Disney traditions of quality, but it is also necessary since each of the four small locomotives makes an estimated 13,500 annual trips around the mile and a half long oval of track surrounding the "Magic Kingdom."

Knott's Berry Farm

In contrast to its neighbor in Anaheim, the railroad at Knott's Berry Farm in Buena Park features authentic, "full-sized" narrow gauge locomotives and rolling stock. This reflects the ideas of park founder Walter Knott, who tried to preserve genuine artifacts from the history of the West. Knott, along with his wife Cordelia, operated a restaurant and food sales business in Buena Park, and began collecting western memorabilia and buildings in order to preserve memories of the "Old West." This collection, arranged as the "Calico Ghost Town," began as entertainment for visitors to the restaurant, but quickly grew to become a tourist attraction in its own right.

When, in the middle of 1951, Walter Knott heard that the Rio Grande Southern Railroad was soon to be abandoned, he realized that some valuable western rail history was in jeopardy of being lost. In July of that year, Knott purchased Locomotive No. 40 from the Rio Grande Southern and had it transported by rail from Colorado to Los Angeles. A few months later Knott purchased a companion locomotive, two parlor cars, and three coaches from the Denver and Rio Grande Western Railroad's narrow gauge line. This equipment was also shipped by rail to Los Angeles and then trucked to Buena Park.

Steam trains began running on a mile and a half oval of narrow gauge track encircling the "Ghost Town" and parking facilities near Beach Boulevard and La Palma Avenue as early as November of 1951. Soon after, Knott purchased the abandoned Hansen freight agency station from Pacific Electric and moved it to the park to be reconstructed as the Ghost Town Depot. A formal "Golden Spike" ceremony was held on January 12, 1952, to officially celebrate completion of what became known as the "Ghost Town and Calico Railway." Following speeches by Knott, Carlton Sills of the D&RGW, and William Jeffers of the Union Pacific, steam train operations began on the "Ghost Town Railway." The popularity of the attraction can be gauged from the fact that over one million patrons rode the trains during their first year of operation at the Berry Farm.

Table A.2:
Locomotives and Rolling Stock of the
Calico and Ghost Town Railway at Knott's Berry Farm

(All equipment is 36-inch gauge)

(A) Locomotives

No.	Name	Wheel Type	Builder	Date	Number	Note
40	Green River	2-8-0	Baldwin	1881	5571	(1)
41	Red Cliff	2-8-0	Baldwin	1881	5731	(2)
464	(none)	2-8-2	Baldwin	1903	21796	(3)

(B) Motor Cars

No.	Built	Engine Mfr.	Body Mfr.	Note
3	12-1931	Pierce Arrow	Pierce Arrow	(4)

(C) Passenger Equipment

No.	Name	Body Type	Builder	Date	Note
B-20	Edna	Business Car			(5)
105	Durango	Parlor	Jackson & Sharp	1880	(6)
310	Silverton Coach		Pullman	1887	(7)
325	(unknown)	Coach	Pullman	1887	(8)
326	(unknown)	Coach	Pullman	1887	(9)
351	Calico	Coach	Jackson & Sharp	1880	(10)

In addition to this rolling stock, Knott's Berry Farm also has a Rio Grande Southern Railroad caboose (No. 0402), and an assortment of ex-D&RGW freight cars.

Notes:

(1) Built as Denver and Rio Grande Railroad No. 40 "Reno," class C-19 (in service 05-1881); renumbered Denver and Rio Grande Western Railroad No. 340 "Green River;" renumbered D&RGW RR No. 400 "Green River;" new steel boiler (1916); sold to Walter Knott (03-1952); shipped to Buena Park and entered service as Calico and Ghost Town Railway No. 40 "Green River" (1952); in service 1988.

(2) Built as Denver and Rio Grande Railroad No. 41 "Red Buttes," class C-19 (in service 08-1881); renumbered D&RG No. 409; new steel boiler (1916); sold to Rio Grande Southern Railroad, renumbered No. 41 "Red Cliffs" (11-1916); sold to Walter Knott (07-1951); shipped to Buena Park and entered service as Calico and Ghost Town Railway No. 41 "Red Cliffs" (11-1951); in service 1988.

(3)   Built as Denver and Rio Grande Western Railroad No. 464, class
       K-27, Vauclain Compound (1903); simpled and converted to
       Walschaerts valve gear; retired by D&RGW (1962); sold to Knott's
       Berry Farm (11-1973); shipped to Buena Park and entered service as
       Calico and Ghost Town Railway No. 464 (05-1974); sold to Genesee
       County, Michigan, Parks and Recreation Commission (1981).

(4)   Built by Rio Grande Southern Railroad with Pierce Arrow engine and
       body (in service 12-1931); rebuilt with GMC motor and Wayne bus
       body (1946); sold to Walter Knott (03-1952); shipped to Buena Park
       and placed into service on Calico and Ghost Town Railway without
       renumbering (1952); withdrawn from service and placed on static
       display (1953); restored and returned to service (1973); withdrawn
       from service.

(5)   Built as Rio Grande Southern Railroad private business car "Edna;"
       renumbered No. B-20; sold to Walter Knott (1952); never used in
       regular service, and presently stored.

(6)   Built by Jackson & Sharp as Denver and Rio Grande Railroad coach
       No. 31 (1887); renumbered Chair Car No. 409 (circa 1890); named
       "Pagosa" (1903); rebuilt as parlor-buffet for use on "San Juan Express"
       (02-1937); sold to Walter Knott (1952); in service 1988.

(7)   Built by Pullman Palace Car Company as Denver and Rio Grande
       Railroad Chair Car No. 310 (1887); sold to Walter Knott (1952);
       renumbered No. 104, and named "Silverton" (1952); original number
       restored (1975); in service 1988.

(8)   Built by Pullman Palace Car Company as Denver and Rio Grande
       Railroad Chair Car No. 325 (1887); rebuilt for use as diner (date
       unknown); rebuilt as chair car (circa 1937); sold to Walter Knott
       (1952); renumbered 102 (1952); original number restored (1975); in
       service 1988.

(9)   Built by Pullman Palace Car Company as Denver and Rio Grande
       Railroad Chair Car No. 326 (1887); rebuilt for use as diner (date
       unknown); rebuilt as chair car (circa 1937); sold to Walter Knott
       (1952); renumbered 103 (1952); original number restored (1975); in
       service 1988.

(10)   Built by Jackson & Sharp as Denver and Rio Grande Railroad Chair Car
       No. 410 (1880); named "Camp Bird" (1902); rebuilt as parlor-buffet
       car for use on "San Juan Express," and renamed "Chama" (03-1937);
       sold to Walter Knott (1952); rebuilt as combination coach-baggage car
       by Knott's, renumbered No. 101, and renamed "Calico" (1952);
       renumbered No. 351 (1975); in service 1988.

(Source: Knott's Berry Farm)

By 1973, the two steam locomotives on the Calico and Ghost Town
Railway were reflecting the wear of two decades of hard service. Both needed
extensive overhauling which would keep them out of service through the busy
summer tourist season. Faced with the need to continue providing rail service

as part of its amusement park's attractions, Knott's management authorized the restoration of Rio Grande Southern Motor Car No. 3, one of the Rio Grande Southern's famed "Galloping Geese." Goose No. 3 had been purchased by Walter Knott in 1952 but had not operated over the Calico and Ghost Town Railway since 1953. It was restored to full operation, however, and performed yeoman service through the summer.

To forestall such a problem from happening again in the future, Knott's arranged with the D&RGW to purchase a retired K-27 "Mudhen" still stored in the railroad's roundhouse at Durango. The locomotive was delivered to Buena Park in November 1974, where work began to restore it to operating condition. The big "Mudhen" was placed into service on May 20, 1974, and operated for several years in rotation with its older, smaller cousins. The following year, 1975, all of the locomotives and rolling stock at Knott's were restored to the color scheme and numbers carried in earlier times. This decision was arrived at by Knott's management to reflect the true value of the rail collection in the preservation of western rail history.

Unfortunately, the big 2-8-2 locomotive, No. 464, was too hard on the Ghost Town Railway's light rail and tight curves, so in 1981 it was sold to the Genessee County, Michigan, Parks and Recreation Commission for use on its "Huckleberry Railroad" near Flint, Michigan, where it remains in use today. As a result of this sale, Knott's acquired a large quantity of ex-D&RGW freight cars, some of which have been rebuilt to accomodate passengers. With these changes and additions, the collection of Rio Grande locomotives and cars at Knott's Berry Farm now represents the most complete set of such rail equipment in operating condition outside the State of Colorado.

After its purchase by Walter Knott, Rio Grande Southern No. 41 was shipped by rail to Union Pacific's East Yard in Los Angeles, where it was photographed before being transferred to trucks for the journey into Orange County, November 1951.
– Union Pacific

A pair of cranes carefully lifts narrow gauge parlor car "Durango" from its flat car to motor trucks waiting to carry it the last few miles to its new home at Knott's Berry Farm, September 1951.
– Union Pacific

B Appendix
Orange County Railroad Stations

This list of Orange County stations includes all known agency (manned) passenger and freight stations. Certain other "named places" mentioned in operating timetables are listed if they had structures to accomodate passengers or freight, even if they were not manned by railroad employees. Pacific Electric's numerous passenger halts, and the passenger stations in Orange County's amusement parks are not listed. Three Southern Pacific agency stations on the Santa Ana Branch, and one Union Pacific agency station on the Anaheim Branch, all lying outside Orange County, are included for completeness.

Southern Pacific

Station	Opened	Closed	Removed	Notes
Downey	1875	1947	by 1968	New depot 1886
Norwalk	1901	1947	by 1969	Frt. only 1875
Whittier	1888	1947	1990	Preserved at new location
Buena Park	1888	1933	1943	
Almond	1886	1930	unknown	Shelter only (orig. Costa)
Brookshurst	1886	unknown	1935	Freight only
West Anaheim	1875	1930	1943	Orig. Anaheim (1875-1899); then Loara (1899-1907)
Anaheim (downtown)	1899	1958	1975	passenger area remodeled 1940s
Tustin Jct.	1899	unknown	unknown	Bench only; renamed South Anaheim 1955
West Orange	1885	1911	1932	Listed on time-tables until 1937
Santa Ana	1878	1960	1971	Orig. at Fruit Street; new depot built at 4th St., 1896

Villa Park	1896	unknown	1940	Orig. Wanda, changed 1919
McPherson	1891	1903	unknown	Agency in packing house
El Modena	1888	see note	1939	Station built, but not manned
Tustin	1889	1938	1944	Burned 1944
Newport Beach	1891	1923	1923	New joint SP/PE station built 1927
Huntington Beach	1903	1971	1977	Orig. psgr. shelter only; PE depot moved to SP site 1942
La Bolsa	1921	1928	unknown	Agency may have closed in 1931
Westminster	1907	unknown	1938	
Los Alamitos	1896	1924	unknown	

Union Pacific

Station	Opened	Closed	Removed	Notes
Whittier	1923	1969	1983	Demolished
La Habra	1923	1956		Owned by city since 1979; now Children's Museum

Southern Pacific's ubiquitous "Standard No. 23" depot appeared throughout the Southwest with minor variations in siding, ornamental detail and orientation. Three stations were built to this pattern in Orange County, the newest, in downtown Anaheim, being built in 1899.
– Lee Gustafson Collection

Station	Opened	Closed	Removed	Notes
Fullerton	1923	1973	1982	Moved to new site; now used as restaurant
Anaheim	1923	1972	1987	Moved to new site; to be preserved

Atchison, Topeka and Santa Fe Railway

Station	Opened	Closed	Removed	Notes
Buena Park	unknown	1963	1963	Orig. Northam
Fullerton	1888	see note		New depot built 1930; Freight agency closed 1989; still used by Amtrak
Anaheim	1888	1972	1987	New depot built 1941
Anaheim (Stadium)	1984	see note		Built by City for use by Amtrak; in use
Placentia	1910	1970	1971	Opened in a boxcar; depot built 1911
Richfield (first)	1887	see note	1892	Not manned; removed for use as house, still standing

Built with an eye toward future growth, Union Pacific's Anaheim Depot was far too large for the amount of traffic it ever saw. This photo shows the station in November 1923, just a few months after the branch line opened.
– Union Pacific photo, John Signor Collection

Richfield (second)	1920	1960	unknown	Renamed Atwood in 1920
Olinda	1902	1930	unknown	
Yorba	1892	1913	unknown	
Olive	1929	1960	1964	
Orange	1888	1971	see note	New depot built 1938; now owned by city for preservation

Typical of the second phase of wooden depots built by the Santa Fe was the Placentia station, built in 1911 to a pattern similar to those in California's San Joaquin Valley. Demolished in 1971, this was the last wooden Santa Fe depot in Orange County.
– W.C. Whittaker photo, John Signor Collection

Typical of the "Carpenter's Gothic" stations built by the Santa Fe along its main line through Orange County in the 1880s was the ornate Santa Ana depot, shown here in 1938 not long before it was demolished to make way for its "Spanish Colonial Revival" successor.
– Lee Gustafson Collection

Santa Ana	1887	1982	1986	New depot built 1939; replaced by Santa Ana Reg. Trans. Center 1986 In use by Amtrak
Aliso (2nd)	1888	1903	unknown	Orig. South Tustin; see also El Toro
Irvine	1910	1968	1973	Renamed Valencia 1965
Irvine (new)	1990	—	—	In use by Amtrak
El Toro	1888	1947	1952	Orig. Aliso (1st) for one year
Capistrano	1894	1968	see note	Renamed San Juan Capistrano 1905; now used as restaurant; Not a passenger agency, but Amtrak still stops here
San Juan	1888	unknown	unknown	Renamed Serra 1905
San Clemente	1931	1938	1964	Not a passenger agency, but Amtrak still stops here

Perhaps the most travelled of PE's Orange County depots was that which served Huntington Beach. Built in 1904 as a "Standard No. 1 Combination" structure (identical to that at La Habra), its open (passenger) end was enclosed to house more office space, and the building itself was moved in 1941 from its original location alongside the Newport line across from the Municipal pier, to Lake Street on the La Bolsa line. The building, pictured here in 1947 at its new location, housed a freight agency until 1977.
– Official Pacific Electric photo, William A. Myers Collection

Pacific Electric

Station	Opened	Closed	Removed	Notes
Huntington Beach	1904	1971	1977	Moved 1942 to SP site on La Bolsa line
Newport Beach	1927	1950	unknown	Joint PE/SP
Garden Grove	1908	1961	unknown	
Santa Ana	1905	1950	1986	New depot 1927
Orange	1923	1963	1986	
La Habra	1909	1971	see note	Moved to new site; preserved
Brea	1909	unknown	unknown	
Yorba Linda	1911	1968	see note	In use as restaurant; little remains of original structure
Fullerton	1917	1938	see note	Used by PE bus service until 1953; in use as restaurant

A typical example of Pacific Electric's widely used "Standard No. 1 Combination" (freight and passenger) station was the La Habra depot, built in 1909 and fortunately now preserved a few yards from its original site. This is one of the last PE depot surviving in Orange County.
– Official Pacific Electric photo by Charles Lawrence, William A. Myers Collection

CAppendix

Chronology of Orange County Railroad Development

1870　The Anaheim Railroad is incorporated to build a line from Anaheim to Anaheim Landing, but no construction is done.

1874　Southern Pacific builds branch from Florence (Los Angeles County) to Anaheim (July to December).

1875　S.P. Anaheim Branch officially opens (January 14). Storm damage closes the new line for several weeks (late January).

1876　S.P. completes its Valley Route line between Bakersfield and Los Angeles, providing Southern California with its first all-rail connection to the rest of the United States (September).

1877　S.P. branch extended from Anaheim to Santa Ana (December 17).

1878　S.P. unsuccessful in attempt to build across Irvine Ranch to San Diego.

1886　Santa Ana, Orange and Tustin Street Railway opens "Depot Branch" in Santa Ana, and horsecar line between Santa Ana and Tustin. Santa Ana and Newport Railroad incorporated to build a wharf at Newport and a rail line to Santa Ana.

1887　Atchison, Topeka and Santa Fe Railway opens line from Riverside to Santa Ana through Santa Ana Canyon (September 15), and from Santa Ana to San Juan (December). Anaheim Street Car Company opens Center Street line, and SA,O&T St. Ry. opens extension to Olive Street in Santa Ana.

1888　AT&SF opens lines from Orange to Los Angeles, and from Capistrano to Oceanside, thus completing last sections of new "Surf Line" to San Diego (August 12). S.P. builds branch from Miraflores (South Anaheim) to Tustin (July). Santa Ana, Fairview and Pacific Railroad builds narrow gauge line from Santa Ana to Fairview (Costa Mesa) (June). SA,O&T opens line to Orange Plaza (first with horsecars, and then in July with the Steam Dummy). Orange, McPherson and Modena Street Railway opens line between Orange and Modena. S.P. fails in second (and last) attempt to cross Irvine Ranch to build to San Diego.

1889　Heavy rains in March cause damage to steam railroads and street railways. Newport Wharf opens (January). Fairview Railroad ceases running (April).

1890   The Santa Ana and Westminster Railroad is incorporated to build from Santa Ana to Westminster. Fairview Railroad abandoned. Construction resumes on Santa Ana & Newport Railway (June). Orange, McPherson and Modena Street Railway abandoned.

1891   SA&N opens (January 12). SA&W builds one-half mile of track on Second Street in Santa Ana (November); public protests end work. Fairview Railroad rails removed.

1893   SA&N purchases incomplete SA&W.

1895   SA,O&T abandons line between Santa Ana and Tustin in October. (The steam dummy line to Orange also suspends service, but is not dismantled.)

1896   S.P. builds a branch from Anaheim to Los Alamitos. The steam dummy between Santa Ana and Orange resumes operation under name of Santa Ana and Orange Motor Road in April.

1897   SA&N builds branch from Newport up the coast to Shell Beach (Huntington Beach) and inland to Smeltzer (near Westminster); line opens (October 7). W. A. Clark builds Orange County's first beet sugar plant at Los Alamitos. The first celery is shipped by rail via the SA&N from Orange County (November). Oil discovered in Olinda district.

1899   W. A. Clark purchases the SA&N (February 1st). S. P. buys SA&N from Clarks (June 14). S. P. also builds downtown Anaheim "loop" trackage. AT&SF builds Olinda branch north from Richfield. Anaheim Street Railway Company abandons last horsecar line in Orange County.

1901   Inter-Urban Railway assumes operation of the Orange steam dummy. The "old" Pacific Electric Railway Company is incorporated.

1903   P.E. line opened to Whittier (November 7). S.P. opens Newland station to accomodate growing sugar beet traffic from farms in the area.

1904   P.E. line opened from Long Beach to Huntington Beach (June 17).

1905   P.E. line opened from Huntington Beach to Newport (August 5), and from Watts to Santa Ana (November 6). P.E. shortens steam dummy operations to a truncated route between Santiago Creek and Orange Plaza.

1906   P.E. opens a local trolley line on Main Street between Fourth and Santiago Creek in Santa Ana. P.E. commences interurban trolley service to East Newport (May 13), and to Balboa (July 4). S.P. crews begin grading Smeltzer-Stanton connection, but work interrupted.

1907   S.P. opens a connection between Smeltzer and Stanton, completing its famous "Orange County Loop Line" via Santa Ana, Newport, Huntington Beach, Stanton and Anaheim (August 15). Daily except Sunday "merry-go-round" mixed train service commences over this line.

1908   P.E. opens service to Pillsbury (2.25 miles east of La Habra). Local trolley service between Santa Ana and Delhi opens.

1909   P.E. opens line between Santa Ana and Huntington Beach. Southern California Sugar Company opens its beet sugar plant at Delhi.

1910   AT&SF opens "Placentia Cut-off" between Richfield and Fullerton
July 1). P.E. sold to Southern Pacific Company (November). P.E. opens
service to Randolph (now Brea) and Yorba Linda. P.E. electrifies S.P.
(ex-S.A.& N.) branch between Huntington Beach and La Bolsa
(December).

1911   P.E. opens passenger service to Stern, east of Yorba Linda. Anaheim
Sugar Company opens its beet sugar plant at Anaheim. Holly Sugar
Company opens its plant at La Bolsa.

1912   S.P. builds freight-only electric spur between Delhi and Dyer south of
Santa Ana; P.E. electrifies the trackage. The Santa Ana Sugar
Cooperative builds its beet sugar plant at Dyer. During this year, sugar
beets and beet sugar products are Orange County's most valuable
agricultural product.

1913   P.E. begins local service on Alamitos Bay-Bay City (Seal Beach) line
(September 12).

1914   AT&SF builds Venta Spur onto the Irvine Ranch. P.E. abandons
steam dummy service to Orange Plaza. P.E. opens all-electric line into
Orange (June 8).

1915   AT&SF operates seven daily passenger round trips through Orange
County on its Los Angeles to San Diego line, and five daily passenger
round trips through Santa Ana Canyon; for the San Diego corridor, this
is the best pre-Amtrak frequency of service. Orange County's most
spectacular train accident occurs near Yorba Station on the AT&SF,
when a runaway oil tank car hits an oncoming passenger train; three
crewmen die, 30 passengers injured (August 4).

1916   Heavy rains in January and February cause major damage to Orange
County rail lines. P.E. does not restore trolley service to Newport until
April. S.P. discontinues its last two steam-powered local passenger
trains between Los Angeles and Santa Ana, although two McKeen cars
continue in service.

1917   P.E. opens passenger service to Fullerton. President Woodrow
Wilson nationalizes the nation's steam railroads (December 20); P.E. is
not affected.

1918   S.P. opens its La Bolsa freight agency.

1919   P.E. discontinues running of its "Triangle Trolley Trip" to Orange
County (August 1). Oil discovered in East Placentia-Richfield
(Atwood) area.

1920   Oil discovered in Huntington Beach (May 24). The Federal
government returns steam railroads to their owners (March). AT&SF
builds new depot at Richfield, and renames this station Atwood.

1921   Union Pacific is authorized to build a branch line into Orange County.

1922   P.E. discontinues passenger service on the Santa Ana to Huntington
Beach line. Greenville to Huntington Beach portion of this trackage
removed at unknown date. Orange County Rock and Gravel Company
begins rail operations in Santiago Creek, near McPherson on S.P.'s
Tustin Branch.

1923   U.P. opens its Anaheim Branch via La Habra and Fullerton, offering twice daily passenger service by "McKeen" rail-motor cars (July 1). S.P. discontinues its last local passenger service in Orange County, the Los Angeles to Anaheim rail-motor trains, and the "Merry-go-round" mixed train (August 12). The beet sugar plants at Delhi and Anaheim are closed. S.P. abandons and removes its ex-SA&N wharf and station trackage in Newport.

1926   P.E. builds freight-only line from Orange to Marlboro (date uncertain). The Los Alamitos and La Bolsa sugar plants close; all remaining production in the county is concentrated at Dyer.

1927   P.E. extends its Balboa line trackage to the harbor mouth to facilitate construction of the North Jetty.

1928   P.E. ends passenger service on the La Bolsa branch.

1929   U.P. ends rail passenger service (using McKeen cars) into Orange County, substituting instead bus service from its new East Los Angeles station (May 15).

1930   P.E. purchases Motor Transit Company and begins converting some Orange County rail services to bus transit. P.E. abandons Santa Ana to Orange rail service although "Marlboro Island" is retained for freight service. AT&SF begins using EMC motor trains to operate local mail and passenger accomodation trains between Los Angeles and San Bernardino through Santa Ana Canyon, and also over the Olive subdivision.

1933   S.P. abandons and removes its steam line from Dyer to Newport Beach and Huntington Beach, and transfers ownership of the La Bolsa line to P.E. exclusively. S.P. also abandons its original Orange County "main line" right of way between West Anaheim and Miraflores to facilitate construction of Manchester Boulevard.

1934   Western Salt Company begins operation of a 24-inch narrow gauge railroad at its evaporation ponds in Upper Newport Bay.

1936   P.E. runs summer-time only parlor car service from Balboa to Los Angeles.

1937   P.E. again operates summer-time only parlor car service between Balboa and Los Angeles under the name of the "Special Club Car Commodore."

1938   Severe rain storm and flooding causes major disruption to rail lines in Orange County (early March). AT&SF begins streamliner service on its San Diego route through Orange County (March). P.E. discontinues rail passenger service on the La Habra-Brea-Yorba Linda and Fullerton lines (January 22), and abandons the trackage between Stern and Yorba Linda. Freight service continues over the remainder of the line. P.E. operates club car "Commodore" between Los Angeles and Balboa in summer months.

1939   P.E. operates club car "Commodore" between Los Angeles and Balboa in summer months.

1940   P.E. discontinues all passenger services on Balboa line, except for one daily round trip franchise run (June 9). P.E. discontinues Seal Beach local line (November 17). P.E. abandons line between Newport and Balboa (November 18), and remainder of "Newport Line" becomes freight only. This is the peak year of acreage planted in citrus in Orange County. Construction of Prado Dam forces AT&SF to relocate several miles of its main line at the east end of Santa Ana Canyon. AT&SF removes Olinda Spur.

1941   AT&SF adds second streamliner trainset to San Diegan pool, increasing service to four daily round trips using streamliners, and one round trip with conventional equipment. P.E. moves its Huntington Beach passenger depot from its old location adjacent to the municipal pier to a new site inland at Lake Street on the La Bolsa line, converting it into a freight agency station only.

1942   P.E. restores club car "Commodore" between Los Angeles and Newport (July 20-September 18). The U.S. Navy builds line from Westminster to new Seal Beach Naval Ammunition Depot. U.S. Army builds "Segerstrom" spur from P.E. at Greenville to Santa Ana Army Air Base at Costa Mesa.

1943   AT&SF double tracks the San Diego line between La Mirada and Fullerton to accomodate increased war-time traffic (May 10). AT&SF opens CTC between Fullerton and Venta (October 22). P.E. restores full passenger service on Newport line (May 2-September 20). "Commodore" operates June 18-September 20.

1944   P.E. restores limited passenger service on Newport line, including "Commodore" (June 19-September 18). AT&SF opens CTC between Venta and San Diego (July 4).

1945   AT&SF opens CTC between Fullerton and Esperanza (April 8); and on Olive District (September 10). P.E. again restores limited passenger service on Newport line, including "Commodore" (June 17-September 15). This is the peak year for citrus shipped by rail from Orange County, 20.9 million boxes.

1946   P.E. revives limited rail passenger service on Newport line (June 17), to augment bus service over Pacific Coast Highway. "Commodore" operates this summer.

1947   P.E. operates "Commodore" service between Newport and Los Angeles this summer.

1948   P.E. operates "Commodore" service between Newport and Los Angeles this summer. S.P. transfers ownership of La Bolsa-Los Alamitos-Stanton trackage to P.E. (freight service only).

1949   P.E. operates "Commodore" service between Newport and Los Angeles this summer. Last club car operates September 9th.

1950   P.E. finally abandons passenger service over Newport line (June 30), although portions retained for freight service. Passenger service to Santa Ana abandoned (July 3), ending passenger trolley service in Orange County.

1951 Knott's Berry Farm receives ex-Rio Grande Southern No. 41 and ex-Denver and Rio Grande Western narrow guage equipment for use on its new "Ghost Town and Calico Railroad."

1952 AT&SF begins using Budd rail diesel cars in San Diegan services through Orange County (May), raising service to six daily round trips.

1953 AT&SF handles 35 trainloads of Boy Scouts to the National Jamboree held on the Irvine Ranch (June). S.P. also handles extra passenger trains, but busses the scouts into Orange County. Reenactment of the "Golden Spike" ceremonies at the Jamboree using ex-Virginia and Truckee Railroad equipment.

1954 S.P. operates its last steam locomotive in Orange County, pulling an enthusiast excursion from Los Angeles to Tustin and Santa Ana (May). S.P. opens the Puente Cutoff, bypassing Los Angeles to speed freight deliveries to Orange County. AT&SF increases San Diegan service to seven daily round trips, matching the previous all-time high prior to 1917.

1955 P.E. abandons its trackage on Fourth Street in Santa Ana, rerouting its freight services via S.P.'s Stanton-Anaheim-Santa Ana trackage. Disneyland begins operating narrow gauge steam trains. AT&SF discontinues its last motor train for local main and passengers over the Placentia Cutoff.

1956 AT&SF replaces rail diesel car passenger service with conventional locomotive-hauled passenger trains following a serious wreck at Redondo Junction in Los Angeles. Service cut to six daily round trips.

1958 P.E. removes its bridge between Seal Beach and Long Beach, finally severing its old Newport line. A Marine Corps jet trainer crashes in front of a southbound AT&SF "San Diegan" near El Toro, fortunately with no major injuries to anyone.

1959 Disneyland begins operating its monorail line.

1962 P.E. abandons its Huntington Beach-Newport Beach freight trackage, and closes the Garden Grove freight agency.

1964 P.E. and U.P. begin joint use of a single track from Colima to Fullerton. (P.E. trackage is used Colima to Laon Junction, U.P. trackage is used Laon Junction to Fullerton.) P.E. abandons its Fullerton Branch from just south of Laon Junction into Fullerton, including the "Welcome Arch" bridge over Harbor Boulevard. Although over 700 passengers ride AT&SF passenger trains daily to and from Orange County stations, cancellation of the U.S. Mail contract causes the railroad to discontinue two round trip passenger trians on the San Diego corridor, leaving only four round trips in service.

1965 AT&SF discontinues one additional round trip on the San Diego corridor through Orange County. S.P. absorbs all remaining P.E. freight services, ending the separate history of the former trolley company.

1966   AT&SF installs Centralized Traffic Control on San Diego line west of
        Fullerton. S.P. abandons and removes the former P.E. trackage between
        Huntington Beach and Seal Beach.

1968   AT&SF discontinues its "Grand Canyon," the last remaining
        passenger train using the trackage through Santa Ana Canyon. Holly
        Sugar purchases S.P.'s historic diesel No. 1000 (built 1939) to switch
        the sugar factory at Santa Ana (Dyer). AT&SF closes Irvine (Valencia)
        freight agency.

1969   Heavy storms cause some damage to Orange County rail lines,
        including washing out S.P.'s Tustin Branch bridge over Santiago Creek.
        S.P. abandons Tustin Branch trackage south of Santiago Creek, thus
        ending service to Orange County's last rail shipper of sand and gravel.
        S.P. closes and demolishes Santa Ana depot (agent moves to P.E. depot
        on Fourth Street).

1970   AT&SF demolishes Irvine (Valencia) depot near Sand Canyon Avenue on
        the Irvine Ranch. S.P. closes the last ex-P.E. freight agencies in Orange
        County (La Habra and Huntington Beach), and moves all remaining
        operations to Anaheim. AT&SF closes Placentia freight agency, as local
        citrus production ends (November 1).

1971   Amtrak takes over ex-AT&SF passenger operations (May 1).
        Turbotrain makes demonstration run through Orange County (August).
        AT&SF demolishes Placentia Depot, its last wooden station in Orange
        County (February).

1973   S.P. abandons and removes the ex-P.E. trackage between Yorba Linda
        and "Brea Chem" (Kraemer Avenue and Imperial Highway).

1976   The American Freedom Train steams through Orange County
        behind ex-S.P. No. 4449, stopping at Anaheim and San Juan
        Capistrano (January). U.S. Navy holds open house at Seal Beach Naval
        Weapons Center (May), and offers rides over its extensive rail trackage.
        Amtrak introduces Amfleet equipment on the San Diego corridor trains
        and increases daily service to four round trips. S.P. abandons its old "La
        Bolsa" line trackage between Huntington Beach and Wintersburg.

1977   Amtrak increases service on the San Diego corridor to five daily round
        trips.

1978   S.P. abandons and removes ex-P.E. trackage between Stanton and West
        Santa Ana (July). County of Los Angeles "El Camino" passenger train
        begins operation through Orange County, providing a sixth daily round
        trip on the San Diego line.

1979   O'Connor Engineering of Costa Mesa ships operating replicas of two
        "Golden Spike" steam locomotives to the Golden Spike National
        Monument at Promontory, Utah. The sugar plant at Dyer, Orange
        County's last such facility, is closed.

1980   Amtrak increases service on the San Diego corridor to seven daily
        round trips.

1982 AT&SF closes Santa Ana freight agency. Bullet train is proposed to run through Orange County between Los Angeles and San Diego. S.P. abandons Tustin branch between Marlboro and Santiago Creek (portion south of Villa Park not used since ca. 1969).

1984 Amtrak and the City of Anaheim open a new passenger station at Anaheim Stadium. Orange County Railway Historical Society founded. AT&SF closes and removes 5-mile Irvine (formerly Venta) Spur onto the Irvine Ranch, marking the end of major agricultural rail shipments originating from Orange County. Orange County Transit District purchases ex-P.E. Santa Ana line right of way between West Santa Ana and Stanton for future rail transit use. Sales tax proposal for transit improvements in Orange County defeated. Bullet train proposal dropped.

1985 New Santa Ana Regional Transportation Center opens (Fall), and Amtrak ceases using old AT&SF Santa Ana depot, which is abandoned.

1986 Amtrak reroutes its "Desert Wind" through Santa Ana Canyon, restoring passenger service over this route.

1987 Amtrak increases service on the San Diego corridor to eight daily round trips and begins "push-pull" operations. AT&SF Santa Ana depot demolished. Ex-P.E. Santa Ana depot demolished. S.P. and U.P. terminate agreement that gave S.P. trackage rights over U.P. line between West Fullerton and Anaheim. U.P. abandons outer end of branch in Anaheim (south of 91 Freeway).

1988 Start of LOSSAN project to upgrade rail, track structure and signalling on AT&SF's San Diego Subdivision in Orange County.

1989 S.P. begins operating freight trains over portion of AT&SF line between Anaheim and Santa Ana; its line between these places is sold to the State of California for widening the Interstate 5 freeway. S.P. offers to sell over 150 miles of branchlines, including some in Orange County, to facilitate public development of rail transit. LOSSAN project completed on AT&SF's San Diego Subdivision in Orange County, to accommodate additional train service. AT&SF closes its last Orange County freight agency, housed in the Fullerton depot, which is sold to City of Fullerton for continued use by Amtrak.

1990 Amtrak and the City of Irvine open a new commuter passenger station at (East) Irvine, adjacent to El Toro Marine Air Station. Additional round trip passenger service between Los Angeles and San Juan Capistrano begun.

D Appendix
Future Transit Use of Railroad Rights of Way

*E*ven though the majority of Orange County's railroad lines continue to function as viable carriers of passengers and freight, regional transit planners have begun to covet these railroad rights of way for possible use as future transit corridors. In particular, the Southern California Association of Governments (SCAG) has studied the suitability of reusing some railroad routes for rail transit, and has concluded that several lines in Orange County should be earmarked for purchase and conversion.

Of these lines, that seen as the most important is the remaining segment of Southern Pacific's West Santa Ana Branch, the former Pacific Electric Santa Ana line. That portion of this route lying south of Stanton has been abandoned for some time and is owned by the Orange County Transit District (although that district recently voted, in a short-sighted act of bureaucratic vandalism, to permit buildings to be built on a portion of the right of way in Garden Grove). North of Stanton, however, rails continue to serve industrial customers as far north as Paramount in Los Angeles County. A transit service operated over this corridor would have the potential to connect the Santa Ana Civic Center with Long Beach, the Los Angeles Central Business District, or Los Angeles International Airport, via the "Red," "Green," and "Blue" light rail lines presently being built by the Los Angeles County Transportation Commission.

It is noted that this route borders or is surrounded by "large medium" to "high" population density residential areas and employment zones, and would serve significant existing and future shopping, commercial, governmental and educational areas, all of which are seen as important traffic generators. SCAG's researchers have also noted that the "West Santa Ana Branch" corridor parallels, and would offer substantial relief to congested freeways such as Interstate 5 (the Santa Ana Freeway), State Route 22 (the Garden Grove Freeway), and Interstate 405 (the San Diego Freeway). Total demand for transit travel along this corridor has been estimated to be as high as 60,000 daily riders, which gives it a high priority among regional transit planners.

SCAG analysts have also concluded that other Orange County branch lines would make good transit corridors. These include: Southern Pacific's Los Alamitos and Stanton-Huntington Beach Branches; the U.S. Navy's Seal Beach Railroad; and Union Pacific's Anaheim Branch. Although rated as of less urgent need, Southern Pacific's Brea Branch (the former Pacific Electric Yorba Linda line) is also identified as of future value to Orange County's transit requirements.

Furthermore, although outside the SCAG study, there has been much public debate over the possible construction of a high speed magnetic levitation passenger railroad from Anaheim to Las Vegas along an all-new corridor. A local system of "transit ways," using monorail or other technologies, would feed into stations along this route.

While SCAG stops short of recommending specific transit technologies, it has evaluated options undertaken elsewhere. To the authors of these volumes, it appears that "light rail" transit may offer the best combination of low capital cost for construction, ease of maintenance, rider carrying capacity, speed, operational flexibility, energy efficiency and low cost of operation. Unfortunately, any type of rail transit other than the existing commuter services along the Santa Fe Railway corridor seems to be very far in the future despite the urgent need for them now. The voters of Orange County repeatedly have failed to approve any funding measures at the polls, and in so doing have left the mistaken impression within the political system that there is no constituency for rail transit in Orange County. Perhaps as a result of this mistaken perception, those politicians responsible for county transit decision making have refused to take the lead to create a master rail transit plan and work towards its implementation. The recent action of County Supervisors permitting the vital West Santa Ana line right of way to be built upon, thus bisecting this important corridor and forestalling rail construction on it for at least twenty years, is just the latest act of folly in a long history of tragically irresponsible decisions.

SELECTED BIBLIOGRAPHY

This list of references gives the sources consulted in the preparation of this book. Where newspapers or serial publications were issued over a series of years, the dates given indicate the span of dates reviewed for this book, not the total span of publication. When a single date is followed by a plus sign, this indicates that selected individual issues were reviewed, beginning with the earliest date shown.

PRIMARY SOURCES

Railroad Documents From Corporate Archives

Atchison, Topeka & Santa Fe Railway Company. Annual Reports. New York and Chicago, 1875-1980.

———. Building Records, AT&SF Ry. System, Los Angeles Division. 1920 + .

———. Car Location Identification Code. ca. 1983.
[Identifies all industrial spurs in Orange County.]

———. Dispatcher's Log, San Bernardino, 1917-1985.
[Also known as "Dispatcher's Trainsheets."]

———. Daily Record of Train Movements, Los Angeles Division. 1936 + .

———. Employee Timetables, Special Rules and Operating Bulletins. 1887-1988.
[Primarily of the Los Angeles and Los Angeles Terminal Divisions, and also of the Southern California Railway, 1887-1904.]

———. List of Officers, Agents and Stations. Various years.

———. Monthly Record of Shipments Handled at Orange Station. 1938-1949.

———. Rules and Instructions Governing Transportation of Freight. 1897.

———. Santa Fe Magazine, 1908 + .

———. Track Charts, Los Angeles Division. 1960, with periodic revisions. [Provides profile, elevations and track features.]

Pacific Electric Railway Company. Timetables. Various years, various lines, 1902-1936.

Southern Pacific Company. *Annual Reports*. New York and San Francisco, 1874-1988.

———. Engineering Department. Los Angeles. Profile Diagrams and Track Records. Various sheets covering Orange County lines. 1918-1985.

———. List of Officers, Agents and Stations. Various years from 1903.

———. Los Angeles Division. Office of the Superintendent. Employee Timetables, Special Instructions and Bulletins. 1874-1988.

———. "Seventy Five Years of Progress: A Historical Sketch of Southern Pacific," by Erle Heath. San Francisco: Southern Pacific News Bureau, 1945. Revised 1955.

———. *Southern Pacific Bulletin*, 1915 + .

———. Southern Pacific Industrial Numbering System. Books for Orange County zones. 1981.

———. Tariffs, Freight Rates and Classifications. San Francisco. 1878, 1894 + .

———. Valuation Department. Right of Way and Track Maps. San Francisco. 1916 + .

Union Pacific Railroad. Employee Timetables and Special Rules, Los Angeles Division. 1923-1988.

———. Office of the Chief Engineer. Condensed Profile. Omaha, Nebraska. No dates.

Privately Held Archival Collections of Railroad Documents

Atchison, Topeka and Santa Fe Railway Company, The. "Construction of the Santa Fe Lines South of Barstow." Undated (ca. 1941), typescript. Document No. RR573:86, "ATSF Files," Kansas State Historical Society, Topeka, Kansas.

———. "History of the Santa Fe Coast Lines, AT&SF Railway." 1940, revised 1980, typescript. Santa Fe Railway Historical Society, Fountain Valley, California.

———. "Santa Fe Railroad. . . History of its Construction, Characteristics of Line, Nature of Country, Kinds and Sources of Commodities Transported." March 1945, typescript. Santa Fe Railway Historical Society, Fountain Valley, California.

Fellows, Richard J. The Magna Collection of the late Ira L. Swett, pertaining to the Pacific Electric Railway and predecessors.

Melching, Ralph. Photographs and documents.

Pacific Electric Railway Company. Engineering Department. "Pacific Electric Railway, Valuation, Inventory and Appraisal as of June 30, 1914, Revised and Updated to 1948; Incorporating a History of all Predecessor Companies and Survey of Lines in Operation to 1948." June 30, 1914, with revisions to 1948, typescript. Golden West Collection, Courtesy Donald Duke.

Santa Fe Railway Historical Society, Fountain Valley, California. Documents and drawings.

Younghans, Raymond. Offical correspondence files, maps, drawings, records and miscellaneous documents pertaining to the Pacific Electric Railway Company.

Interviews

Anthony, Dick. Southern Pacific locomotive fireman in Orange County, 1908. Interview by Stephen E. Donaldson.

Carlson, Amil. Southern Pacific locomotive fireman in Orange County, 1903-05. Interview by Stephen E. Donaldson.

Connell, Stanley R. Santa Fe Railway trainman. Interviewed by George Sefcik, August 1, 1989.

Drenk, Robert. Santa Fe Railway Assistant Manager, Refrigerated Freight Operations. Interviewed by George Sefcik, August 10, 1989.

Dyer, Jasper. Santa Fe track foreman in Orange County, 1935-1962. Interview by Stephen E. Donaldson.

Leahy, Ed. Southern Pacific freight agent in Orange County, 1960-1980. Interview by Stephen E. Donaldson.

Leichtfus, George. Santa Fe operator/agent at Orange Station, 1914-1971. Interview by Stephen E. Donaldson.

Lindsey, Claude. Santa Fe passenger agent in Orange County, 1904-1955. Interview by Stephen E. Donaldson.

McFadden, Arthur J. Son of the President of the Santa Ana & Newport Railway. Interview by Stephen E. Donaldson.

Thompson, Joseph P. Santa Ana & Newport, and Southern Pacific brakeman, 1891-1899. Interview by Stephen E. Donaldson.

Weaver, Ed. Southern Pacific locomotive fireman in Orange County, 1910-1950. Interview by Stephen E. Donaldson.

SECONDARY SOURCES

Periodicals (Journals)

Barsness, Richard W. "Iron Horses and an Inner Harbor at San Pedro Bay, 1867-1890." *Pacific Historical Review*, (1965): 289-303.

———. "Railroads and Los Angeles: The Quest for a Deep Water Port." *Historical Society of Southern California Quarterly*, 47 (September 1965): 379-394.

Batman, Richard D. "Orange County, California: A Comprehensive History." *Journal of the West*, (1965): 425-445.

Best, Gerald M. "Early Steam Suburban Railroads in Los Angeles." *Railway & Locomotive Historical Society Bulletin*, no. 99 (1958): 8-25.

Best, Gerald M., and David L. Joslyn. "Locomotives of the Southern Pacific Company." *Railway & Locomotive Historical Society Bulletin*, no. 94 (1956): entire issue.

Harloe, Bart. "Early Railroads in Orange County." *Pacific Historian*, 23, no. 3 (Fall 1979): 43-49.

Dodge, Richard V., and R.P. Middlebrook. "The California Southern Railroad." *Railway & Locomotive Historical Society Bulletin*, no. 80 (May 1950): 10-45.

Hoyt, Franklyn. "The Influence of the Railroads in the Development of Los Angeles Harbor." *Historical Society of Southern California Quarterly*, 35 (1953): 195-212.

———. "The Los Angeles & San Pedro: First Railroad South of the Tehachapis." *California Historical Society Quarterly*, 32 (1953): 327-348.

———. "The Los Angeles & Independence Railroad." *Historical Society of Southern California Quarterly*, 32 (1950): 293-308.

———. "The Los Angeles and Pacific Railway." *Historical Society of Southern California Quarterly*, 34 (1952): 260-270.

———. "The Redondo Railroad." *Historical Society of Southern California Quarterly*, 36 (1954): 130-137.

———. "The Los Angeles Terminal Railroad." *Historical Society of Southern California Quarterly*, 36 (1954): 185-191.

———. "The Los Angeles & San Gabriel Valley Railroad." *Pacific Historical Review*, no. 20 (1950): 227-239.

———. "San Diego's First Railroad: The California Southern." *Pacific Historical Review*, no. 23 (1954): 133-146.

Lesley, Lewis B. "The Entrance of the Santa Fe Railroad into California." *Pacific Historical Review*, no. 8 (1939): 89-96.

———. "A Southern Transcontinental Railroad into California: Texas & Pacific vs. Southern Pacific, 1865-1885." *Pacific Historical Review*, no. 5 (1936): 52-60.

Miller, Willis H. "Competition for the Ocean Trade of Los Angeles." *Economic Geography*, 13, no. 4 (October 1937): 325-333.

Montgomery, W.F. "Pioneer Lumber Dealers in Los Angeles." *Historical Society of Southern California Quarterly*, 24 (1924): 66-80.

Periodicals (Magazines and Other Serial Publications)

Best, Gerald M. "San Bernardino Steam Dummy Lines." *The Western Railroader*, no. 280 (May 1963): 1-17.

Donaldson, Stephen E. "The Santa Ana & Newport Railway." *The Western Railroader*, no. 395 (1968): 1-14.

Engineering News-Record, 1886

McKinney, Kevin. "Surfside Streamliner." *Passenger Train Journal*, 13, no. 11 (May 1982): 28-35.

The Official Guide to the Railway and Steam Navigation Lines of the United States, Puerto Rico, Canada, Mexico and Cuba. Issued monthly. New York: National Railway Publications Company. 1875-1970 (selected issues).

Railroad Gazette, 1886

Railway Age, 1886

Street Railway Journal, 1902

Periodicals (Newspapers)

Anaheim Gazette, 1870-1910
Colton Semi-Tropic, 1877-1878
Daily Alta California (San Francisco), 1884-1891
Fullerton Tribune, 1890
Highland (California) Messenger, 1911+
Huntington Beach News, 1905-1930
Huntington Beach Post
Los Angeles Herald, 1874
Los Angeles Star, 1870-75
Los Angeles Times, 1890
Press & Horticulturist (Riverside), 1890
Newport News, 1913-1940
National City Record, 1890-1891
Orange County Herald, 1890-1903
Redlands Citrograph, 1891
Redondo Courier, 1892-1893
Riverside Press, 1880
San Bernardino Guardian, 1870-1880
San Bernardino Weekly Times, 1878-1888
San Diego Union, 1870-1891
San Pedro Times, 1905-1906
San Francisco Bulletin, 1880 (in Bancroft Scraps)
San Francisco Guide, 1896-1899
Santa Ana Blade, 1888-1925
Santa Ana Bulletin, 1899-1907
Santa Ana Daily Press, 1890-1891
Santa Ana Herald, 1878-1905
Santa Ana Morning Dispatch, 1904
Santa Ana Register, 1904
Santa Ana Standard, 1888-1905
South Riverside Bee, 1888-1891
Southern California (Anaheim), 1873-1874
Wilmington Enterprise, 1875

Books

Armour, Samuel. *History of Orange County, California*. Revised edition. Los Angeles: Historic Record Company, 1921.

Armstrong, John H. *The Railroad-- What It Is, What It Does*. Omaha, Nebraska: Simmons-Boardman Publishing Company, 1977.

Bloodgood, Hedwig L. *Biographical Sketches from West Anaheim*. Anaheim: Anaheim Historical Society, 1984.

Bail, Eli. *From Railway to Freeway: Pacific Electric and the Motor Coach*. Interurbans Special 90. Glendale, California: Interurban Press, 1984.

Best, Gerald M. *Ships and Narrow Gauge Rails: The Story of the Pacific Coast Steamship Company*. Berkeley, California: Howell-North, 1964.

Butler, W.E. *Down Among the Sugar Cane: The Story of Louisiana Sugar Plantations and their Railroads*. Baton Rouge, Louisiana: Moran Publishing, 1980.

Cleland, Robert Glass. *The Irvine Ranch*. San Marino, California: The Huntington Library, 1966.

Chamberlain, H.A. *The Picture Story of Buena Park, From Coyotes to Cityhood*. Buena Park, California: Buena Park City and Historical Society, 1971.

County of Orange. *Bienvenidos Al Canon de Santa Ana: A History of the Santa Ana Canyon*. Anaheim, California: County of Orange, Environmental Management Agency, 1976.

Cox, Thomas R. *Mills and Markets*. Seattle: University of Washington Press, 1974.

Crump, Spencer. *Ride the Big Red Cars: How the Trolleys Helped Build Southern California*. Los Angeles: Trans-Anglo Books, 1962.

Diebert, Timothy S., and Joseph A. Strapac. *Southern Pacific Company Steam Locomotive Compendium*. Huntington Beach, California: Shade Tree Books, 1987.

Dodge, Richard V. *Rails of the Silver Gate: The Spreckels' San Diego Railroad Empire*. San Marino, California: Golden West Books, 1960.

Duke, Donald. *Pacific Electric Railway: A Pictorial Album of Electric Railroading*. San Marino, California: Pacific Railway Journal, 1958.

Duke, Donald, and Stan Kistler. *Santa Fe: Steel Rails Through California*. San Marino, California: Golden West Books, 1963.

Dumke, Glen S. *The Boom of the Eighties in Southern California*. San Marino, California: The Huntington Library, 1944.

Dunscomb, Guy L. *A Century of Southern Pacific Steam Locomotives, 1862-1962*. Modesto, California: The Train Shop, 1963.

Friis, Leo. *More Than the Golden Spike: The Life of David Hewes*. Santa Ana, California: Friis-Pioneer Press, 1968.

———. *Orange County Through Four Centuries*. Santa Ana, California: Pioneer-Friis Press, 1965.

Guinn, James M. *Historical and Biographical Record of Southern California*. Chicago: Chapman Publishing Company, 1902.

Hanft, Robert M. *San Diego & Arizona: The Impossible Railroad*. Glendale, California: Trans-Anglo Books, 1984.

Hofsommer, Donovan L. *The Southern Pacific, 1901-1985*. College Station, Texas: Texas A&M University Press, 1986.

Lee, Ellen K. *Newport Bay: A Pioneer History*. Newport Beach, California: Newport Beach Historical Society, 1973.

Lindley, Walter, and J.P. Widney. *California of the South: Its Physical Geography, Climate, Resources, Routes of Travel, and Health Resorts.* New York: Appleton, 1888.

Locklin, D. Philip. *Economics of Transportation.* Homewood, Illinois: Richard D. Irwin, 1972.

Long, Raphael. *Red Car Days: Memories of the Pacific Electric.* Interurbans Special 92. Glendale, California: Interurban Press, 1983.

Marquez, Ernest. *Port Los Angeles: A Phenomenon of the Railroad Era.* San Marino, California: Golden West Books, 1975.

Marshall, James. *Santa Fe, The Railroad That Built an Empire.* New York: Random House, 1945.

McAfee, Ward. *California's Railroad Era, 1850-1911.* San Marino, California: Golden West Books, 1973.

McCall, John B. *The Doodlebugs.* Dallas: Kachina Press, 1977.

McMillan, Joe. *Route of the Warbonnets.* Woodridge, Illinois: McMillan Press, 1982.

Meyer, Samuel A. *Fifty Golden Years: A History of the City of Newport Beach, 1906-1956.* Newport Beach, California: The Newport News, 1956.

Miller, Edrick J. *A Slice of Orange: The History of Costa Mesa.* Costa Mesa, California: The Costa Mesa Historical Society, 1970.

_____. *The Hayburners of Orange County.* Costa Mesa, California: The Costa Mesa Historical Society, 1978.

Myers, William A. *Iron Men and Copper Wires: A Centennial History of the Southern California Edison Company.* Revised edition. Glendale, California: Trans-Anglo Books, 1986.

Myrick, David F. *The Railroads of Nevada and Eastern California.* 2 volumes. Berkeley, California: Howell-North, 1962-63.

Nadeau, Remi. *City Makers: The Story of Southern California's First Boom, 1867-1876.* Los Angeles: Trans-Anglo Books, 1965.

Orange County Historical Society. *Orange County History Series.* 3 volumes. Santa Ana, California: Orange County Historical Society, 1931-32.

Osterman, Joe. *Fifty Years in "Old" El Toro.* Fullerton, California: Sultana Press, 1982.

Parker, C.E., and Marilyn Parker. *Indians to Industry.* Santa Ana, California: Orange County Title Company, 1963.

Plat Book of Orange County, California: Compiled From County and Government Surveys and the County Records. Los Angeles: H.S. Crocker Company, n.d. (ca. 1910).

Pleasants, Mrs. J.E. *History of Orange County.* Los Angeles: J.R. Finnell and Sons, 1931.

Rolph, George Morrison. *Something About Sugar: Its History, Growth, Manufacture and Distribution.* San Francisco: J.J. Newbegin, 1917.

Sherman, Henry L. *The History of Newport Beach.* Los Angeles: Times-Mirror Press, 1931.

Signor, John R. *Southern Pacific-Santa Fe: Tehachapi.* San Marino, California: Golden West Books, 1983.

Strapac, Joseph A. *Southern Pacific Review.* Huntington Beach, California: Pacific Coast Chapter, Railway & Locomotive Historical Society, 1977.

_____. *Southern Pacific Review.* 1981.

_____. *Southern Pacific Review, 1952-1982.* 1982.

_____. *Southern Pacific Review, 1983-1985.* 1985.

Swanner, Charles D. *Santa Ana-- A Narrative of Yesterday, 1870-1910.* Claremont, California: Saunders Press, 1953.

Swett, Ira L., editor. *Cars of the Pacific Electric Railway.* Volume 1, *City and Suburban Cars.* Interurbans Special 28. Los Angeles: Interurbans, 1964.

_____. *Cars of the Pacific Electric Railway.* Volume 2, *Interurban and Deluxe Cars.* Interurbans Special 36. Los Angeles: Interurbans, 1965.

_____. *Cars of the Pacific Electric Railway.* Volume 3, *Combos, RPOs, Box Motors, Work Motors, Locomotives, Tower Cars, Service Cars.* Interurbans Special 37. Los Angeles: Interurbans, 1965.

_____. *Lines of the Pacific Electric: Southern District.* Interurbans Special 16. Los Angeles: Interurbans, 1959.

_____. *Official Car Records, Pacific Electric Railway Company.* Interurbans Special 38. Los Angeles: Interurbans, 1964.

_____. *Tractions of the Orange Empire.* Interurbans Special 41. Los Angeles: Interurbans, 1967.

Swett, Ira L., and James W. Walker, Jr., editors. *Lines of the Pacific Electric: Southern and Western Districts.* Interurbans Special 60. Revised edition. Glendale, California: Interurbans, 1975.

Veysey, Laurence R. *A History of the Rail Passenger Service Operated by the Pacific Electric Railway Company since 1911, and by its successors since 1953.* Interurbans Special 21. Los Angeles: Interurbans, 1958.

Wager, Charles H., et al. *Industrial Traffic Management.* Washington, D.C.: The Traffic Service Corporation, 1973.

Waters, L.L. *Steel Trails to Santa Fe.* Lawrence, Kansas: University of Kansas Press, 1950.

Walker, Chard. *Railroading Through Cajon Pass.* Denver: Prototype Modeler, 1978.

Wellington, Arthur M. *The Economic Theory of the Location of Railways.* Revised edition. New York: John Wiley & Sons, 1904.

White, John M., Jr. *The Great Yellow Fleet.* San Marino, California: Golden West Books, 1988.

[Wilson, John Albert.] *History of Los Angeles County California, with Illustrations Descriptive of its Scenery, Residences, Fine Blocks and Manufactories.* Oakland, California: Thompson & West, 1880; reprint edition, Berkeley, California: Howell-North, 1959.

Worley, E.D. *Iron Horses of the Santa Fe Trail.* Dallas: Southwest Railroad Historical Society, 1965.

Brochures, Pamphlets, Limited Circulation Publications

Illustrated History of Southern California. Chicago: Lewis Publishing Company, 1890.

Land of Sunshine: Southern California. Los Angeles: H.E. Brook, 1893.

Nelson, Tom. *Pacific Railroad Society Fortieth Anniversary Compendium.* Los Angeles: Pacific Railroad Society, 1977.

Orange County, California: History of its Soil, Climate, Resources and Advantages. Santa Ana, California: Board of Trade, 1897.

Orange County and the Santa Ana Valley. Santa Ana, California: Chamber of Commerce, ca. 1899.

Southern California Standard Guide Book. Los Angeles: Los Angeles Times, 1910.

The Herald Pamphlet. Los Angeles: 1875.

Tribune Annual and Southern California Statistician. Los Angeles: Los Angeles Tribune, 1890.

Published Reports and Proceedings

Parsons, Brinckerhoff, Quade & Douglas. *The Los Angeles-San Diego Corridor.* Santa Ana, California: Parsons, Brinckerhoff, Quade & Douglas, 1983.

Smith, Wilbur, and Associates, et al. *Los Angeles-San Diego (LOSSAN) State Rail Corridor Study.* Sacramento: California Department of Transportation, 1987.

Southern California Association of Governments. *Railroad Right-of Way Evaluation Project.* 3 volumes. Los Angeles: Southern California Association of Governments, 1989.

Dissertations, Theses and Other Academic Papers

Askevold, Robert J. "Population Growth and the Railroads: A Case Study of Three Orange County Cities." Unpublished manuscript at Special Collections Library, California State University, Fullerton.

Freidricks, William Ben. "Henry Huntington and Metropolitan Entrepreneurship in Southern California, 1898-1917." Ph.D. dissertation, University of Southern California, 1986.

Holcomb, C.E. "History of the Railroad in Orange County." April 4, 1952, typescript. Special Collections Library, California State University, Fullerton.

Hoyt, Franklyn. "Railroads in Southern California, 1868-1900." Ph.D. Dissertation, University of Southern California, 1951.

Veysey, Laurence R. "The Pacific Electric Railway Company, 1910-1953: A Study in the Operations of Economic, Social and Political Forces Upon American Local Transportation." B.A. Thesis, Yale University, 1953.

GOVERNMENT DOCUMENTS AND ARCHIVES

Federal Government

U.S. Congress. House. *Report on Newport Harbor, California*. 60th Congress, 1st session. Document No. 82. 1907.

_____. *Reports on Examination and Survey of Newport Harbor, California*. 63rd Congress, 1st session. Document No. 42. 1913.

[U.S.] Engineer Office. *Survey of Newport Harbor, California*. San Francisco, 1888.

INDEX

* Denotes photograph.

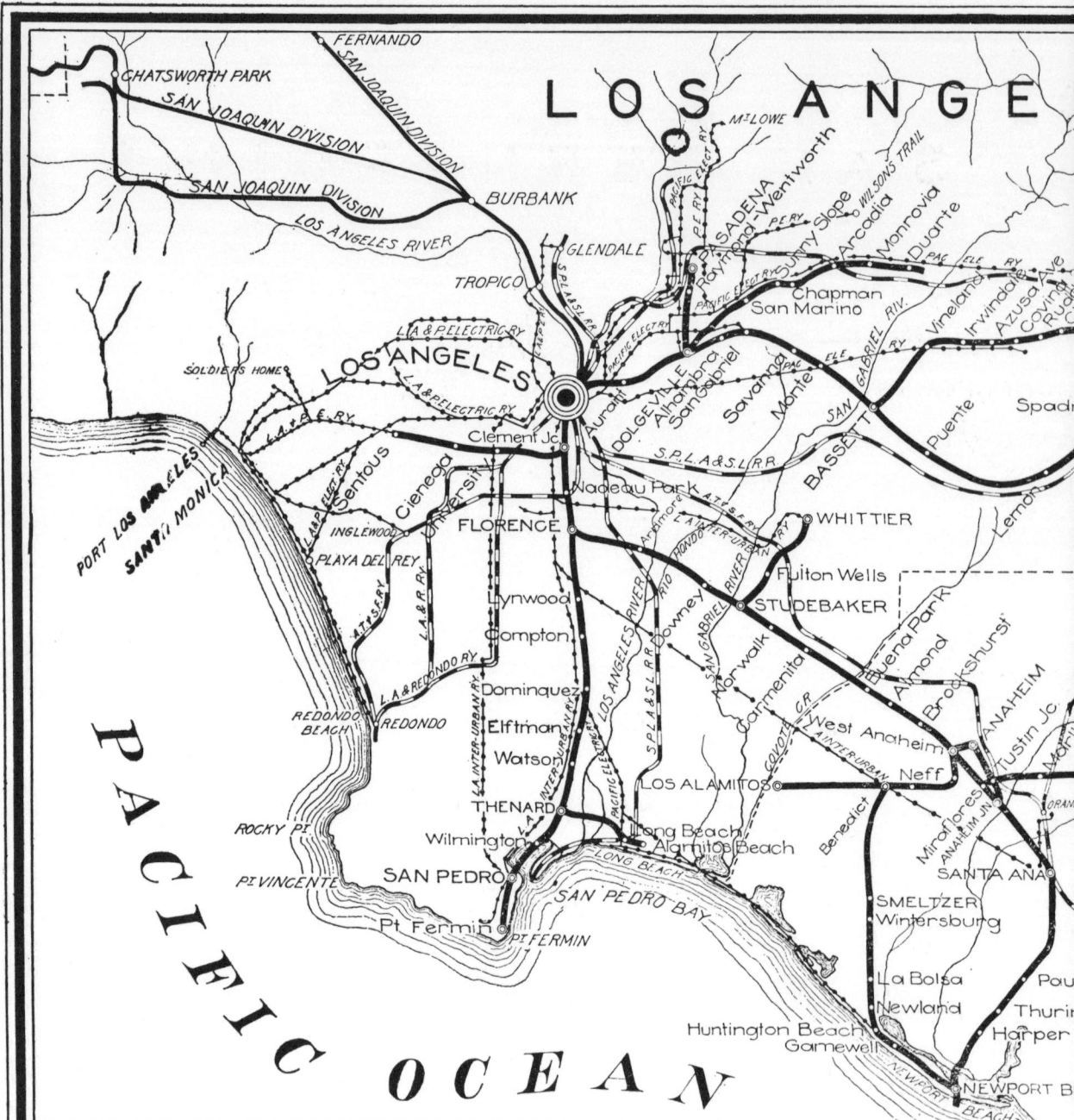

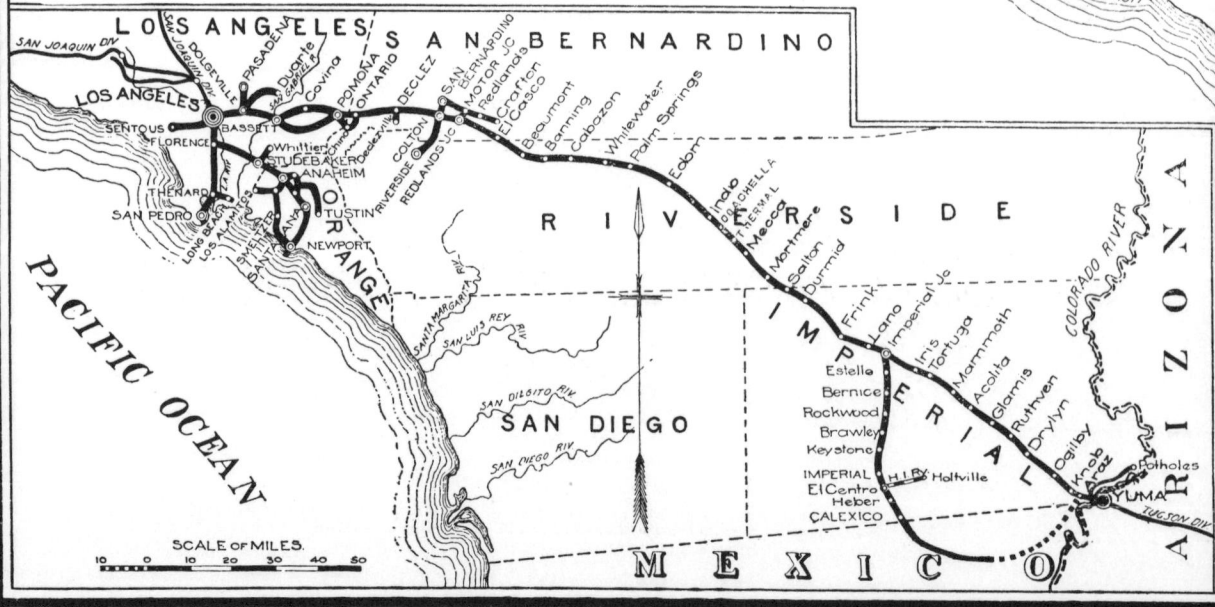